HOW TO GET PUBLISHED IN INDIA

HOW TO GET PUBLISHED IN INDIA

Your go-to guide to write, publish and sell your book
With tips and insights from industry experts

Meghna Pant

BLOOMSBURY
NEW DELHI • LONDON • OXFORD • NEW YORK • SYDNEY

BLOOMSBURY INDIA
Bloomsbury Publishing India Pvt. Ltd
Second Floor, LSC Building No. 4, DDA Complex, Pocket C - 6 & 7
Vasant Kunj, New Delhi 110070

BLOOMSBURY, BLOOMSBURY INDIA and the Diana logo are
trademarks of Bloomsbury Publishing Plc

First published in India 2019
This edition published 2019

ISBN: PB:- 978-93-88271-06-6; eBook:- 978-93-88271-08-0
10 9 8 7 6 5 4 3 2
Typeset in Adobe Jenson Pro by Manipal Digital Systems
Printed and bound in India by Thomson Press India Ltd.

To find out more about our authors and books visit www.bloomsbury.com
and sign up for our newsletters

Contents

Foreword

WE ALL have a story to tell. Almost everyone wants to be a writer and every writer wants to be a bestseller. Almost no one knows how.

Storytelling is the most primal mode of human communication. It is at the heart of all families, societies and cultures. We write stories because we share a love of words, a love for the imagination, and a love for understanding the world we inhabit. We overcome our darkest fears and our biggest obstacles to be able to write. And then ... we begin to question ourselves: *Is my writing really that good? Will I ever finish my book? Will someone publish my book? Will anyone read my book? Will anyone like my book?* Our darkest fears become our biggest obstacles. We don't know how to finish writing our book. We don't know how to get our book published. We don't know how to sell our book. We give up.

Yes, publishing a book is an intimidating, frustrating and confusing endeavour. If you are an outsider, then it is even more so. Who will you turn to for answers? Who will hold your hand through this muddling process? It's lonely being a writer, isn't it? There's no one to really help you, is there? Trust me, I know. I spend a decade teaching myself how to write. I spend another decade teaching myself how to publish and sell my books. I didn't have a degree in literature or marketing. I didn't have mentors or connections. All I had was passion, dedication and tenacity – dollops and dollops of it. After years of rigorous and soul-wrenching work, I published novels, short-story collections and non-fiction. Through those long years I kept hoping someone would write a book like this for the Indian market. I know it would have made my journey as an author a lot easier.

Ever since I became a published author in 2012, I've received queries from people around India asking me how they can get published. They think there's a secret I know and they don't. Well, I'm sorry – there are no easy tricks or gimmicks. But if you're willing to put in the work, with patience, devotion and a love for your craft, there are insights, methods and advice in this book that other famous writers, editors, publishers and insiders in the publishing industry haven't shared with you before.

To begin with there's good news and bad news. Whether you're writing mythological fiction, self-help, historical accounts or murder mysteries, there has never been a better or worse time to be an author. Why? Because it's easy to get published but difficult to sell. Authors are fighting for the reader's attention not only with other authors, but also with the latest outrage on Twitter, the fakest news cycle on WhatsApp, the newest feature on Facebook, the craziest Instagram photo of Taylor Swift, and the most WTF moment by an Indian politician. We are questioning whether people are even reading books any longer. Has the long-awaited death of the novel finally happened? Is Indian publishing over? Have you missed your chance to write your magnum opus? No way! Our country is full of opportunities for first time authors if you know where to look. Today we have three generations of English-speaking Indians who are hungry to read. They are particularly hungry to read in English. Ours is the only country with a growing rather than declining English language readership! On top of that, the closed ranks of the literary world have opened up. Today, India is the sixth-largest book publisher in the world, with hundreds of publishers printing thousands of books each year. Major foreign publishing houses are setting up operations in India year after year. A person can publish a book within minutes thanks to the advent of self-publishing and digital publishing. This means that no matter what you're writing—and even if you're not a Bollywood personality, a controversial politician, a celebrity cricketer, a dietician to the stars, or a spiritual guru—you can still get published!

As a new writer the biggest obstacles you'll face will be to finish your manuscript, find a suitable publisher, and build a large base of readers. In the following chapters, I've shared with you writing tools, publishing tips and marketing tricks that will give you everything you need to get going. I'm not going to lie to you, every author needs a little bit of luck, a little fairy dust to hit the big time; everything else I'm going to help you with in the coming pages – from brass-tacks and publishing hacks: how to develop as a writer, how to sell your novel to publishers, and how to market your novel.

The book is divided into four chapters.

The first chapter focuses on the craft of writing: the grammar, language, dialogue, the settings, character development, exposition, plot, theme, narrative style, the conception of an idea, formatting your manuscript and editing. You will learn how to live like a writer, and deal with issues like personal finance and writer's block, along with avoiding common mistakes made by first-timers.

The second chapter takes you through the basics of what to do with your manuscript. Getting a book published is the black hole for many aspiring writers. In this chapter, you will learn how to pitch your manuscript to publishers, write a killer synopsis, how to frame that difficult query letter, how to put together an enticing submission package, how to identify the right agent for your book, how to identify the right publisher, how to get out of the publishers' slush pile, and how to deal with rejection. Going behind the scenes, you will learn what to expect in a publishing contract, what happens after you sign a contract, the most common setbacks and how you can work around them. We'll be looking at how to publish in different genres and with different types of publishing houses, along with striking out independently and self-publishing, in brief, getting your book the best publisher it deserves.

In the third chapter you will discover the secret to marketing your book successfully and learn everything you need, including social media, public relations, reviews and launches. Learn what ingredients go into writing a bestseller. Develop a marketing plan. Do you need a website? Do you need a book trailer? Do you need a book launch? Get in touch with some of the best practices and tools in book marketing today, and learn how to sell your book like some of India's bestselling authors. In a country where less than 2% of books find their way to a bookstore, you'll learn how your book can make the cut and find that elusive reader.

In the final chapter, masters of the trade, writers who have published to literary acclaim and commercial success in India and the rest of the world, as well as publishers and agents who have brought extraordinary talent to the fore, share their journey, their struggles and their victories, and reveal their trade secrets published together here for the first time.

While I have tried my best to keep all the information up-to-date and timely, there may be some changes and gaps due to the rapid pace with which things develop in publishing and the world. Always follow up with your own research, online search, and checks. Keep up with what's happening in the field you wish to join.

While this book is primarily for those who write in English, I have covered regional languages to the extent possible. The hegemonic role of English in Indian literature has been a bone of contention, for others, and me, especially since India is a land of plurality and diversity. The real taste of India, its very essence, lies in the nooks and crannies, remote or inaccessible places that carry a rich contextual weave of stories. While regional languages and authors are not being adequately represented and hitting the bestseller lists, their time is coming. Due to our diversity in languages, literature will be read and written in major languages like Hindi, Marathi, Malayalam, Bengali, Telugu, Urdu and

Tamil, as well as regional languages. Till that time, please bear with the information I have at hand.

If I've missed something—as I'm sure I have—do forgive me. I've done my best, as should you with whatever you're writing.

Writing, publishing and marketing a book will possibly be one of the toughest things you'll ever do. But when you've done it, there's no better high than a reader sending you a message saying: 'I stayed up all night reading your book.' So stay the courage, my friend.

I wish you well in your writing career, and look forward to reading your book soon.

Meghna Pant

CHAPTER ONE
WRITING

There is nothing to writing. All you do is sit down
at a typewriter and bleed.
— *Ernest Hemingway*

PART ONE:
Writing Tips

What's Your Genre?

THE FIRST question you'll be asked when you introduce yourself as a writer is, "What type of book do you write?". By this they mean the genre. Before anything else, identify what kind of an author you are and in what genre you write.

What is your genre? The genre is the categorization of your story. It's where it'll in a bookshop. It's how it'll be marketed and sold. It's how it relates to the books you read.

Indian authors write, as authors world over do, in several genres. Commercial fiction by its name tends to sell the most copies. Within commercial fiction, romance is the most popular one where authors like Chetan Bhagat, Durjoy Datta, Preeti Shenoy and Sudeep Nagarkar rule the roost. Authors like Anuja Chauhan, Advaita Kala, Yashodhara Lal, Kiran Manral and Swati Kaushal have also made a mark. Mythology continues to attract lakhs of readers with Amish Tripathi, Devdutt Pattanaik, Christopher Doyle, Anand Neelakantan and Kavita Kané notching the bestseller lists. Mysteries and thrillers are popular with authors like Ashwin Sanghi, Ravi Subramanian, Vikram Chandra, Manjiri Prabhu and Manreet Sodhi Someshwar occupying a hallowed distinction in these ranks. Literary fiction is the bulwark of authors like Salman Rushdie, Arundhati Roy, Amitav Ghosh, Rohinton Mistry, Jerry Pinto, Vikram Chandra, and Chitra Banerjee Divakaruni. Sci-fi, fantasy and horror find few takers so far, though these have seen breakthroughs with authors like Samit Basu, Arnab Ray, Indrapramit Das and Shweta Taneja. The era of mass-market books has brought in new genres of campus novels, college romances and crime thrillers. Historical, mythological and religion-based books have also gained traction.

Non-fiction includes self-help, autobiographies, history, travel-writing, memoir, finance, management and corporate books, penned by stalwarts like Ramachandra Guha, Amartya Sen, Gurcharan Das, Radhakrishnan Pillai, Rashmi Bansal and Shiv Khera.

Graphic novels like *Persopolis* and *Maus* are rare with one of the pioneering ones being *Corridor* by Sarnath Bannerji and even the memoir form which is huge internationally and includes bestsellers like *Kitchen Confidential* and *When Breath Becomes Air* to name a few, is taking a much longer time to come of age in India.

Celebrity autobiographies, romance and non-fiction tends to sell better than literary fiction, though that gets the most review space, and worse off yet are short stories, poetry and translated fiction. Still, write what you need to write, not what you think will sell – after all we can all think of exceptional successes in every genre. It's almost impossible to time the publishing market and game the book business. Readers aren't fools.

Keep in mind that publishers have annual targets, and certain limitations and notions. They do not publish all genres, even if they're written well. Therefore, while the West has genres like cli-fi, bizarro and minimalism, in India many Indian readers prefer a slightly more traditional approach to these. What sort of book do you want to write? When you describe it to people, what are the comparisons you will use? Where do you see it sitting in a bookshop? What sort of scope do you have in mind? Is your book going to be a trilogy, is it going to be a collection of short stories? Are you more drawn to fantasy or realism, perhaps magical realism?

Narrow down three to five ideas for a book and focus on them. Spend time with the idea, develop a storyline and try to realise its potential. You could think that if romance sells, you'll do that, but unless it's the book you're burning to write, chances are it'll slip under the radar since there's a lot of competition there.

Ultimately you don't pick your genre, your genre picks you. Don't fit your writing to a genre. Write the story that you want to tell.

Get The Setting Right

THE SETTING in a story is the environment that your character inhabits. It is the time, circumstances and location in which the story takes place. It's hard to try to write anything without knowing and really seeing your setting, and if an author writes a book without telling you anything about the setting, that too is done to elicit a reaction from the reader.

This is what I consider before writing a story:

1. Time – When is the story taking place (period, year, time, date)?
2. Place – Where is the story taking place?
3. Tone – What is the feeling that you want your story to evoke? Is it funny, sad, thoughtful, thrilling, or frightening?
4. Social Conditions – What do people wear? How do they talk? What are their customs? What does their daily life look like? A word of caution: these details need to be shown, not told. Be subtle.

In non-fiction, as well, you must give the reader something to land on. Be specific with locations and numbers in non-fiction. Saying, "I interviewed farmers in a village," is different from saying, "I interviewed fifty-seven cotton-growing farmers in the arid village of Anagola, located in the Mandya district of the southern state of Karnataka."

Be specific. Crosscheck facts. Being vague in non-fiction can be maddening for the reader.

Find The Point Of View

POINT OF view (POV) is the angle from which the story is told. It is the window to your character and her world. Everything that you include in your novel—the dialogue, the action, the narrative—will be determined by the POV. It is the single most important aspect of telling a story, fiction or non-fiction. It grounds the reader and helps them get their bearings, in relation to the story, so they can lose themselves in it.

Before you begin to write your story, you must establish the POV you'll be using. Will your book be in the first person or will it be in the third person? Will you be telling the story from one character's perspective? Or will you narrate your story through the eyes of multiple characters? Many first-time authors tend to use the viewpoint of one or two central characters, so they can fully develop their POV and feel comfortable, rather than dealing with the challenge of trying to inhabit multiple voices.

Start out slowly. Get to know your main character. Know her the way you'd know your best friend: her background, education, personality, flaws, rituals, habits. You don't have to put all these details in your manuscript but knowing them means that they'll be hinted at and lurk in the background of everything that you do write.

Know her language. Think of your genre when picking a POV. For example, if you're writing a romantic novel, then while there may be subplots involving other people, basically you've got to get the voices of your romantic couple right.

Now let's take a look at the different kinds of POVs:

1. First Person – This is the 'I/Me/We' perspective. The narrative is told either by the protagonist, or by a character who interacts closely with the protagonist. The reader experiences the story through the protagonist's eyes and knows only what she knows or feels. Some great fiction and non-fiction books written in first person are *The Great Gatsby* (F. Scott Fitzgerald), *Twilight* (Stephenie Meyer), *The Hunger Games* (Suzanne Collins), *The White Tiger* (Arvind Adiga), *The Blind Lady's Descendants* (Anees Salim), *Hangwoman* (KR Meera), *The Bell Jar* (Sylvia Plath), City of Djinns (William Dalrymple) and *We Should All Be Feminists* (Chimamanda Ngozi Adichie).

2. Second Person – This is the 'You' perspective. This POV makes the reader the central character and is fairly rare. Some great successes written in the second person are Jay McInerney's *Bright Lights, Big City*, and Mohsin Hamid's *How To Get Filthy Rich In Rising Asia* and *The Reluctant Fundamentalist*.

3. Third Person – This is the 'He/She/They' perspective. The most popular POV, you'll find it in a variety of books from classic to contemporary, including *Pride and Prejudice* (Jane Austen), *The God Of Small Things* (Arundhati Roy), *The Lives Of Others* (Neel Mukherjee), *A God In Every Stone* (Kamila Shamsie), *In Custody* (Anita Desai), and *The Subtle Art Of Not Giving A F*uck* (Mark Manson). Third person can be limited or omniscient. Limited is when the narrator presents the perspective of just one character, so the reader knows only what that character knows, like *Harry Potter* (J.K. Rowling). Omniscient is when the all-knowing narrator moves from character to character, and gets into the head and heart of each one. Information is provided, but its interpretation is left to the reader. *Lord Of The Rings* (JRR Tolkien), *The Ramayana* (Valmiki), *The Mahabharata* (Ved Vyasa), *A Fine Balance* (Rohinton Mistry) and *Game Of*

Thrones (George Martin), have all used different versions of this POV.

There are, of course, many novels that break all these rules and mix-up the POV. For example, William Faulkner's *As I Lay Dying* has alternating multiple first person narrators. *The Hours* by Michael Cunningham has multiple, alternating third person limited point-of-views, since its three protagonists span a century. *The Hungry Tide* by Amitav Ghosh switches between third person and first person. *Kafka On The Shore* (Haruki Murakami) switches between second person and first person. You will be able to effectively use unconventional structures only once you develop as a writer. Till then, sticking to the first or third person POV is probably your safest bet.

Develop The Plot

It was on Facebook that Sheba realized her mother was a sad woman.

The US Embassy had denied her mother a visa to visit, not that she had money to buy a ticket that would cost her five month's of groceries. Sheba didn't want to go back, fearing deportation when she tried to return. They hadn't met each other in years. In this time Sheba's old life had slipped away from her like a snake shedding skin. A distance had grown and stayed. Now she looked at the profile pictures her mother had posted—baby Sheba in her arms, Sheba taking her first dip in the pool, Sheba at her sixth birthday party, Sheba riding a pony, Sheba at the airport bidding her only family, her mother, goodbye to study in America—and contrasted them with her mother's wall posts— 'Eating alone in the dark' or 'Can't hear the TV with the guns outside'. That life, her former life, seemed unreal to Sheba, as she sat in her studio apartment on the Upper East side, went to work for Goldman Sachs on Wall Street, and wore the ring Peter had given her for their engagement. She remembered that morning, nine years ago, when news of Saddam's fall had trickled in, and her widowed mother had pawned her jewelry, so Sheba could get out of Iraq.

There was a way that Sheba could bring back her mother into her life. She clicked on the button 'Confirm Friend' and became her mother's first Facebook friend.

THE PLOT is the building block of the narrative. It's the story's soul. It reveals the planned and logical sequence of events in a story, and has to have a beginning, middle and end. In a short story or poem, you will typically write only one plot so that the reader can reach a heightened moment more quickly. In a novel and non-fiction many plots can converge and diverge. In flash fiction (less than 1000 words), like the story I've written above, a story is so short that it can generally have only one plot. Such stories demonstrate how you can combine all elements of a plot in just two hundred words or less.

Many writers have a clear idea of the plot, down to the last detail, before they begin writing their book. Others start to write their book with just an idea of the plot. They begin with the opening line and allow the interaction of the characters to lead them to a logical movement of events. They let the story grow and allow the plot to take shape from an organic situation. It doesn't matter how you begin to write the story, just keep in mind that every narrative is made up of a sequence of events that must move in a logical and convincing order.

These are the five essential parts of plot:

1. Exposition – This is the beginning of a story where the characters and the setting are revealed.

2. Rising Action – This is where we see the main character in conflict. The story will now become complicated. There are two types of conflict:

   a   External – A character struggles with an outside force, against violence, society, interaction with other characters, or circumstance.

   b   Internal – A character struggles with herself, against her choices, her ideas of right and wrong, her urges and desires, her pain, her failures, her mistakes or drawbacks.

   Conflict is essential to the plot. Without conflict there is no plot.

3. Climax – This is when the story reaches a turning point. It is the highest point of interest in a story. The main character is seen

facing her biggest danger and no resolution seems to be in sight. At this point, the reader's interest must be piqued, wondering what will happen next.

4. Falling Action – During this part of the story the reader begins to understand the consequences of the main character's actions. Conflicts get resolved. Events begin winding down.

5. Denouement – This is the final resolution of the story, where you bring the story to a close. The conflict is resolved, the main events are untangled, the loose ends are tied, and the book is concluded.

Build Characters

Dr Dohare is a man of average build in his early forties. The two most noticeable things about him were his thick glasses, through which his eyes seem to bulge, and a weak chin.

— *Avirook Sen, Aarushi*

DO YOU remember the stories that you most love? If you think carefully you'll recall that each of these stories have a character(s) who moved you. Some of these characters may have been created two hundred years ago, like Mr Darcy, who remains the pin-up man for women even today. They can occupy a world you've never inhabited, like Atticus Finch from *To Kill A Mockingbird* who lived in the deep south of America a century ago. As a reader, you feel that you know these characters as you would a good friend. You care about them and are invested in their life. Think of Mowgli, Harry Potter, Estha-Rahel, Mohun Biswas, Jane Eyre, Saleem Sinai, Swami, Lucky Santangelo and Agastya Sen. These characters were authentic, genuine, and relatable. They were either believable because they behaved like real-life people or they were people who you want people to be like. Character building is important in both fiction and non-fiction.

When you write you must do it so plausibly that *you* begin to believe that your characters actually exist. Strange as it sounds, I feel as if my debut novel's characters—Amara, Biji,

Baba, Riya and Lalit—are actually out there somewhere, living their lives in a parallel realm.

The story of the book is the story of the central character(s). This means that the character's story drives the novel. But who are these characters? The protagonist is the main character of your book; the hero or heroine, if you may, who will drive everything in your book. The antagonist is the villain who will oppose the protagonist. The villain is not always outright villainous, like Ravana, but the antagonist, like the aunt in PG Wodehouse comedies, or Baby Kochamma in Arundhati Roy's *The God Of Small Things*. This villain also does not have to be a person; it can be a government or the weather or a disease, for example. Aside from the central character(s), you could also have many supporting characters. They will not occupy the primary storyline, but they will add depth to the protagonist to reflect what she needs.

While writing your character(s), you must also bear in mind these standard writing tools that are used the world over:

1. Plot – Plot is the character in action.
2. Readers – Readers will care about your novel only when they care about your characters. They will not read your novel because they want the world to be saved. They will read your novel because they want your protagonist to survive.
3. Character Introduction – Roughly speaking and keeping in mind that all of this comes with exceptions, try to introduce your main character before page 10. A premise will buy the interest of your reader for about 30 pages. After that, your protagonist will take the book forward.
4. Character Interview – Do a character interview before writing her down. Ask the following questions, and more of your own:
   i.   Where does she live?
   ii. In what era does she live?
   iii. What is her occupation?
   iv. What is her personality?
   v.   What does she look like?

vi. What is her age?

vii. What is her background: her family, friends, education, socio-economic status, upbringing etc.?

viii. What is her motivation? What does she want most from life?

ix. How do others react to her?

x. What's at stake for her? (The risk of failure must be big though within the context of the story, so it could be loss of life or it could be successfully stealing a policeman's helmet)

xi. What are her weaknesses?

This interview is a way to familiarize yourself with your character. Most of this information will not make its way directly into the book, but it will strengthen your story.

5. Character Backstory – Give your character a backstory. Why do we care about Dexter, a blood spatter analyst who kills people in the book by Jeff Lindsay? Because he has a heart-wrenching backstory, which makes us think of him as a crusader and not criminal.

6. Character Name – The name of the character defines the story. Your character must have an appropriate name contextualizing her personality, setting or story. Think of Howard Roark, the undisputed hero of *The Fountainhead* (Ayn Rand). His name contains the words 'hard' and 'roar' underlining the steely character that he is. Character names connote many things: their personality, their ethnic background, the period in which they live, and even who they will become. If you name your protagonist Ganja then don't be surprised if the reader expects him to be a druggie. If you give your characters monikers, like calling the bad guy Ravana and the good guy Ram, it will make them caricaturish. The etymology of character names is something you must pay careful attention to. Ravana, for example, means 'a loud wail'. Severus Snape translates to 'severe' in Latin, summing up the character's temperament. Draco translates to 'a terrifying

beast that spits fire', and Malfoy translates to 'bad faith'. Clearly, one of the authors who gave unforgettable character names is J.K. Rowling.

Be wary of giving your characters similar sounding names. Readers don't tend to read past the initial of a name so it will leave them confused: was that Mira, Mita or Mina? Also, your character's name must correspond to the era in which they live. If you name a female character Padmavati, but she's from 2019, it will seem out of context. If you're really stuck with naming your characters (a common problem among writers, believe me), check baby name books or Facebook. Pay careful attention to the names of people you meet. You never know where inspiration strikes!

7. Character Development – Develop your main character. Make her lively and imperfect. Make her realistic and human. Let her do contradictory things, like a schoolteacher who hates kids. Your character can have one or two stereotypical characteristics, like a stingy Gujju or a loud Punjabi, while also being an individual and complex person who is developing and growing. Think of Railway Raju from *The Guide*, a corrupt tour guide who becomes a holy man. Your story is real only if your character is real. Don't use genre as an excuse to exclude a strong main character. Even books about vampires have a Bella. Even books about wizards have a Harry Potter.

8. Character Conflict – In the first act of your story give your character an occasion to rise to, something that'll let the reader get to know her, while also revealing something about her. Your character has to struggle. She had to fight some odds, whether it's internal—a personality issue—or external. In the second act the reader must be invested in the character even as she reaches a new understanding of the conflicts(s) she is facing. This must be the foundation for the rest of your book. There has to be a wall that she has to break. By the end of the novel she has to have undertaken responsibility and a personal growth journey.

The reader must see the character fight back and resolve her conflicts. Think Jo March, Elizabeth Bennet, or Anna Karenina.

9. Character Rescue –Try to resist the temptation to spoon-feed your reader details about the character or rescue your character(s). It robs them of satisfaction. Your main character, in particular, has to face failures and/or setbacks. Her struggles and victories have to be intrinsic to the plot. She has to earn her ending, happy or not.

Involve The Five Senses

Good writing is weaving a tapestry of such vivid imagery that the reader can see the image in front of her. When an author can evoke sensations in the reader, not the fact that something is cooking, but the sight, smell, sound, touch and taste of a favourite food being cooked, you know it's good writing.

The best way to ease your reader into your story is to trigger all or most of the five senses. What are the five senses? Sight, sound, smell, taste and touch. Readers don't want you to spell out the imaginary world that you've created for your character. They want to experience that world. They want to see, hear, smell, touch and taste that world.

So, how do you create these mental pictures for the reader? The best way to describe what you're seeing is to first visualise it … in your mind. An image must first come to your head. You must see it clearly. Only then can you use sensory details while transcribing a scene to the page. Only then can you take the reader along. If you want to describe the sea in Mumbai, or an army camp in Sikkim, or a small temple in Bhopal, you have to first see it exactly for what it is.

Suppose you're describing this small temple in Bhopal. You must have a clear picture of everything about the temple. You must know the way Ram's statue tilts slightly to the left, the way the incense smells, the trembling ring of the bell, the ray of sunlight falling on the priest, the sweet taste of the prasad and the cold marble floor below your feet. You must see the white paint on the temple wall. You must zoom in and see the part where the paint has chipped off.

You have to enter the imaginary world of your story with all your senses. It takes effort, yes. This is what distinguishes a good writer from a bad one.

Show Don't Tell

SHOW DON'T tell is the oldest rule in the writer's rulebook. But what does it mean? Simply put, it means that a writer must show a moment without telling it. The writer must create mental pictures so that the reader can infer things instead of having things spelt out for her. The reader must be involved in the book such that she can deduce facts instead of passively taking in information. The writer does not have to tell the reader what to think, she has to tell the reader what to think about.

Too much telling is sometimes an indication that you're eager to jot down a lot of the story as quickly as possible. Avoid rushing through your text. Don't use shorthand to tell the reader something that you should be showing. Slow down. Articulate, don't insinuate.

Another rule: the less adjectives or adverbs you use as a crutch, the richer your descriptions will be. When you write descriptions using details and imagery, your writing will have more depth and dimension. Say, I write—"Sameera was a *beautiful* woman." This will mean little to the reader since everyone's idea of beauty is different. If I write—"When Sameera entered the restaurant all heads turned towards her in admiration. The waiter gave her the best seat in the house. The bartender sent her a free cocktail."—I have made it amply clear that Sameera is a beautiful woman, without using a single adjective. The same rule applies for clichés. Instead of writing—"When they stepped outside in *the dark rainy* day they saw a tiny figure standing outside Arav's gate. It was Kanika. They ran up to her."—I write—"When they stepped outside they could *discern* a tiny figure standing outside Arav's gate. They *switched on the patio light*. It was Kanika, soaked to the bone and shivering. *They forgot their umbrellas* and ran up to her." See the difference? I've shown that it's dark and rainy without saying it.

Don't overdo this, obviously. Every single sentence in your book cannot be a description, unless you want to create a novel that no one will read.

Another way to show but not tell is to use foreshadowing. Give the readers warning signs of the things to come without revealing too much. The dramatic principle Chekhov's Gun states that if there's a gun in your book at some time a bullet must be shot See how cleverly Ernest Hemingway foreshadows death in the opening line of his novel *A Farewell To Arms*: "The leaves fell early that year."

Show your reader that you can write, don't tell them that!

Nail The Dialogue

WE USE it every single day, yet dialogue is the one aspect that most writers get wrong. They use too much of it or too little. They pepper it with the wrong language or use it as part of the narrative. But there is a trick to getting dialogue right: keep it simple. Dialogue is neither a Shashi Tharoor tweet nor is it a rambling WhatsApp exchange between teenagers. Dialogue in a book has to be written in the way the character speaks. It has to sound natural. It has to communicate something. It doesn't have to be grammatically correct as long as it exemplifies how the character speaks, but it has to be short and straightforward.

A problem with dialogue that is unique to Indian writers is that the vocabulary, the syntax, the rhythms, the idioms, the jargons and the registers of speech in our regional languages are different from the language in which we are writing or translating: English. So, we either overcompensate—using gentrified Babu English that sounds pallid or inauthentic—or we spoof the language into a mangled parody like Hinglish. The gap between reality and text has to be narrowed so that the character's form of expression is closer to the ground.

Dialogue serves many purposes in a book. It has to either take forward the plot or reveal something about the character. Let's use an example from Ayn Rand's *Fountainhead* Instead of writing, "Howard is a stubborn fellow," Rand showed us who

Howard Roark is by using dialogue, as demonstrated in this exchange between the Dean and him (Chapter One, Page 17):

> "Do you mean to tell me that you're thinking seriously of building *that way*, when and *if* you are an architect?"
> "Yes."
> "My dear fellow, who will let you?"
> "That's not the point. The point is, who will stop me?"

Bang on.

Now ... to the technique. One of the best aspects about dialogue is that there's no need to get creative outside the quotation marks. You don't have to write 'she shouted' or 'she exclaimed' after every quotation. Keep it simple. Use 'she said, he said'. This is the only time as a writer when you can get away with being *less* creative.

Another little trick I learnt over the years is that the writer need not directly answer a question. This means that the answer to a 'yes or no' question does not need to be a yes or no. It can be another question, or a change of topic—something that tells us what the answer is, while also telling us something larger about the characters and their situation.

Before you begin writing your masterpiece, take a moment to think about the gender of your protagonist, since you'll have to write and think from that viewpoint. Know the stylistic differences between your characters. Know how voices will change as per the location, era and milieu of your novel. As per the standard rules of writing, when you're writing female characters you can use more personal pronouns (I, You and We), more adjectives, more emotion, and less facts and numbers. A woman will be more likely than a man to state a preference with a question and be decisive in an apologetic way, while a man will make a demand without hesitation and be unafraid to be aggressive. Think these stereotypes are unbefitting for the 21st century? I thought so too. But, surprisingly (and pitifully), the way men and women speak has not changed at all. The proof is in the pudding, or in the sentences below:

"I'm so sorry that we can't come to the hospital today, sweetie."

"We will reach the hospital tomorrow, 5 pm, not today."

Notice the stylistic differences? You'll immediately be able to tell which gender is speaking in either sentence. Take note. Better still, be the one to change the rules. For it's time for a new order, isn't it?

Don't Overwrite

BACK IN 1999, I began my first short story with this opening line: "Like alienisms the doorbell transmitted through Shambu's malleus, incus and stapes, ribbing him parsimoniously and then mocking him decadently." Is it surprising that no one has ever read the rest of that story?

Let's admit it: none of us can be a Shashi Tharoor. It's an exasperating farrago of truth, but if you use words like 'provincial consciousness' and 'sardonic loneliness' in modern writing, you'll probably not attract many readers. In fact, you'll alienate your reader. A reader must be able to trust your voice. And, for that, your voice must be relatable. Your language must speak directly to the reader.

So—don't use a big word where a smaller word will do the job. Don't write convoluted and muddy sentences. Don't overwrite. Don't write like a Writer with a capital 'W'. Don't bury your gems in excess baggage. Dump the thesaurus. In fact, if you need to find a word in a thesaurus, then you're not doing it right. Capture an emotion or a place without using a single big word.

If there are times in your book where the voice doesn't seem quite right, or where the language is wobbly, simplify it. This is typically an indication of an early draft, of trying to get the story down. When you revise, pay special attention to the words you use. Avoid language that shows off. Choose archetypes over stereotypes. Avoid hyperbole. Avoid clichés like 'a dark stormy night' (we all do it, I know, but don't go overboard). In literary fiction try to keep similes i.e. figures of speech that use 'as' and 'like' to a minimum. For example: 'Shalini is as fiery as a *krantikaari*.' Be similarly careful with the use of metaphors i.e. figures of speech that compare to something. For example: 'Shalini is a *krantikaari*.' Try to say the same thing in a different way. Avoid archaic words like 'abet' and phrases like, 'Pooja felt embalmed by the glow of the firelight,' unless there's a stylistic choice behind them. Such mistakes will be like *haldi* stains on your collar: they will be noticed.

You'll have to pay careful attention if you're writing commercial non-fiction, since you're an expert trying to explain complex ideas to a non-expert. See how simply Malcolm Gladwell explains the title of his book *The Tipping Point*: "The tipping point is that magic moment when an idea, trend, or social behavior crosses a threshold, tips, and spreads like wildfire." Keep it simple. Keep out the jargon. Think of yourself as a doctor. A doctor will not tell you, "You had myocardial infarction." She will tell you, "You had a heart attack."

No matter what genre you're writing, strive for clarity, relevance and concision, such that transparency follows. Lean towards understatement. This doesn't mean that you can't write beautiful descriptions, even in non-fiction. Using vigorous language, strong verbs, the active voice, as well as sensory and concrete details. will bring a story alive on the page.

Write in the way that you speak. Write simply. Write from your heart. Write to touch the heart and soul of the reader. Set your talent free, give it life.

Don't Forget To Edit

HAVE YOU ever wondered what authors mean when they say that they're done with their first draft? The first draft is basically the first copy of your book. It means that you've got the structure of your story, non-fiction narrative, or short story collection down in place. Your first draft, as is normal for a new or seasoned writer, will not look like much. In fact, it will probably be embarrassingly badly written, but thankfully you're the only one who'll get to read it. At this stage you must limit self-criticism or you'll end up taking a year to finish writing even one paragraph. While the first draft can take you months or years to put together, at least you've finished what you started. This is your first victory as a writer. Congratulations!

However, do not mistake your first draft for your final book. That will come together after many revisions. Once your first draft is complete, you'll go back to rewrite and edit it. This will be your second draft. Since you have the plot down, this is the time to fix the bits that don't work. Focus on your content, flow, form, spelling and grammar. There are many mistakes that writers (even the most experienced) make while writing. Some of these mistakes are so common, particularly in our Hinglish language, that we don't even know that they're wrong. After that, depending on your dedication and tenacity, you can revise your book several times, thus creating many drafts. I know authors who have written twenty or more drafts of their book, and some who've stopped at two. No guesses for who makes for a better writer. That said, you can literally keep editing forever, so stop once you feel the manuscript is at its best.

After your second or X-number draft, take time out. Ideally, you should not look at your book for a one-month window, so you can actually forget most of what you've written, and come back to the chopping board unafraid to get rid of phrases or characters that you love, if they do not necessarily belong in your book. Set a timeline that suits you. Even a one-week time out will help you see your text with new eyes.

Begin revising. Now's the time to let loose your inner critic. Do a read aloud of your manuscript. Read it out to yourself or to your dog Tommy, but don't miss a word. Hearing your words out loud will give you a sense of how they'll sound to the reader, while also helping you find the rhythm in your flow, things in language that don't work, and sections that don't ring true. It will help check the voice of your book and flaws in the plot. If you're more tech savvy, you can use the Voice Dream Reader, a text-to-speech app that reads text out loud. It is accessible on iOS and Android mobile and tablet devices. Amazon offers the Read Aloud with Voice Over app. There are other options, like TalkButton and NautralReader. To keep yourself updated with similar apps, search for phrases like 'text to speech' or 'read to me' on your app store.

It helps to print out your entire manuscript and do good old-fashioned hand edits. While I've stopped this method since I'm eco-friendly, I know it's easier to spot mistakes on paper than it is on a screen. Read line-by-line and word-by-word. Find awkward sentences and typos. Cover part of the paper so that you can only see one line at a time. Use a red pen to highlight mistakes and make changes. Don't stop till your entire manuscript is covered in red.

Once your edits are done ask a trusted reader: a friend, family member or author buddy to read your copy and give you feedback. A fresh pair of eyes will more likely spot mistakes and discrepancies, and point out what bits are not working. Don't show your work to more than one or two people, or you'll end up confused and overwhelmed with excessive feedback.

I'm often asked in my writing workshops when to stop editing. As writers, you'll rarely be a hundred per cent satisfied with your work. So, when do you know you're done? This is what I tell all my students: it's like falling in love; you just know. Trust your voice. If you reach a stage where you're mouthing the words to your book, you're sick of your book, you feel that you can no longer look at your book (and this is not because you're lazy), then you're done. Hooray!

If you don't enjoy editing—and some authors don't—you can always hire book consultants or book doctors. These folks will edit or proofread your book for you, as per your requirement but it's still an interactive process and you should be making all the major decisions here. You can find many professional editors online, on websites like Upwork and Fiverr. Before hiring an editor know the editor's job. Your editor must act as both your best friend and worst enemy. Your editor must be gentle but brutal, well-meaning but unbiased. Get an editor who will take out the time to understand your book and you as an author. They have to be able to scour through tone, style, consistency, plot holes and character development. They have to tweak your work and guide you into converting your book from a good one to a great one.

If you don't have a big budget, then ditch the professionals and get the editing done from college students who are studying literature, or young freelancers looking for projects. While you can get editors for as less as 20 paisa per word, try to work out a hybrid deal like say 5 paisa per word for editing and 25 paisa for every correction. You can expect to spend Rs 20,000-30,000 for a 350-page book. Keep in mind that your editor can make or break your book, so don't just hand it over to someone because they're available and affordable.

If you'd rather not spend on editors at all, then go online and use free proofreading softwares like Polish My Writing, Grammarly or After The Deadline. These are lifesavers for writers around the world.

Your words are what define you as an author. If your manuscript is speckled with errors, you will lose credibility as a writer. Make sure to edit well.

Editing Hacks

USE THIS checklist when you're editing. Of course, you can break all the rules - and many people successfully have - but if you're starting out, this may help get you going.

1. Writing is rewriting.
2. Write tightly.
3. Write clearly.
4. Add depth and dimension.
5. Check your grammar.
6. Spell check.
7. Check punctuation and spacing.
8. Proofread.
9. After your final draft, do a printout and read-aloud edit.
10. After your final edit, do the last edit.
11. Have someone else read your writing.
12. Replace an unnecessarily long word with a simpler word, when possible.
13. Replace an unnecessarily long paragraph with a shorter paragraph.
14. Kill your darlings.
15. Write using sentences of different lengths.
16. Avoid crutch words (words that you use too often).
17. Avoid adverbs (words ending with the suffix –ly, like gently, or words like very).
18. Avoid gerunds (words ending with the suffix –ing, like walking, or ending with –y like happily).

19. Limit the time frame (no more than a month for a short story).
20. Limit the main characters, and keep it at two for a short story.
21. Have a strong close by repeating a theme i.e. using the same opening and ending sentence, using a recurring motif, ending with something cryptic, or asking a question.
22. Focus on the reader's viewpoint, not your own.
23. Your reader should notice the message and not the messenger.

PART TWO:
Formatting Tips

Format Your Manuscript

BELOW ARE some basic formatting tips for manuscripts that are used around the world. Remember, you'll still have to customise your manuscript according to the submission guidelines of an agent or publisher.

1. Save your manuscript as a Word document in .doc.
2. Your font must be black.
3. Use 12-point Times New Roman.
4. Use double-spaced line spacing. In Word, select your text. Go to Menu > Format > Paragraph > Line Spacing > Double + Special > First Line.
5. Indent each paragraph with one tab. In Word, select your text. Go to Menu > Format > Paragraph > Indentation > Left > Type 0.5. Do not indent the first paragraph of a new chapter, or one that comes after a sub-header, or one that comes after a bulleted or numbered list. Do not leave one-line spaces between paragraphs.
6. Set the same margin for each page. In Word, select your text. Go to Menu > Format > Document > Margins > Type 2.54 cm for Top, Bottom, Left and Right > Type 0 for Gutter > Type 1.25 cm for Header and Footer.
7. Insert a page break after each chapter. In Word, place the cursor at the end of a chapter. Go to Menu > Insert > Break > Page Break.
8. Use a single space after every period and between words.

9. Use UK English since that's the industry standard in India. In Word, go to Menu > Tools > Language > English (UK).
10. Use "double quotation marks" for all quotations. Use 'single quotation marks' only for "quotations 'within' quotations." Make sure that commas and periods are within quotation marks (","." not ",".").

How To Structure Your Book

STRUCTURE IS everything for a good story. How do you structure a story? First, you must get organised. Put all your creative research and inputs in order—the notes, the story ideas, the character interviews, the title options, character names, plot points, favourite words, favourite lines etc.

Then, you must get ready to write down the synopsis. A synopsis is the outline of your book. It's handy to write a chapter-by-chapter synopsis of your book before you begin writing it. This way you will not get stuck in the middle of your novel, or realise that you've missed a major plot point forcing you to rewrite your book from scratch. If you're writing non-fiction, then your synopsis is an expansion on your table of contents. A synopsis will help to take your book from a basic idea to a concrete story. For example, if you want to write a book about how a man foils a terrorist plot, but you don't know how he will go about doing this, writing down the book in parts, bit-by-bit, through your synopsis, will help you concretize the idea.

Writing a synopsis is hard work. Are you ready?

Read the example below of the chapter-by-chapter synopsis I wrote for my first novel *One & A Half Wife*. It took a lot of work, yes, but it gave my book direction, depth and, as the story kept evolving, I came back to the synopsis as a reference point. Trust me, it was worth every hour spent.

P.S. I've removed the summaries of the last few chapters in case you plan to read it!

EXAMPLE OF A CHAPTER-BY-CHAPTER SYNOPSIS:

Chapter 1: When fourteen-year-old Amara Malhotra's Green Card fails to arrive on time, her domineering mother, Biji, consults the most famous parrot astrologer in their hometown of Shimla. Much to Biji's chagrin, the astrologer predicts that the Green Card will come but Amara's marriage will fail. He secretly gives Amara an emerald stone as keepsake. By evening the Green Card arrives. Biji and Baba – Amara's father – decide to leave for America.

Chapter 2: Biji's rich and successful younger brother, Dua Mama, greets them at the Newark Airport and drives them to their new home in Edison, New Jersey. Amara loves her new house till they go over to Dua Mama's house, five minutes away, which looks like a palace. Amara's excitement at seeing her beautiful cousins, Riya and Tina – whom she hasn't met in seven years – dampens when they treat her with indifference.

Chapter 3: Under the shadow of Dua Mama, the Malhotra family settles into a middle-class life in America. Amara starts attending high school but feels lost among the sophisticated students, a cute boy with straw legs named Bob, and the American accent she cannot follow. She doesn't want to disappoint Baba and Biji – who have pinned their American Dream on her – so she makes a plan to help kick start their American Dream.

Chapter 4: Amara's plan is to make Riya – who Biji insists will make Amara meet eligible Indian boys – notice her. Since they study in the same high school, Amara goes to school dressed up in Riya's discarded clothes and homemade makeup. Riya makes fun of her, in front of Bob – and Amara realizes that she can never be a Riya.

Chapter 5: Humiliated, Amara turns her attention to studies and eventually attends a state university. Here she grows out of Riya's shadow and befriends Stacy, her vivacious accounting classmate who wants to be anything but an accountant, and who introduces Amara to McDonald's and boyfriends. After college Amara's parents want her to continue living with them, so she starts working at Dua Mama's accounting firm.

Chapter 6: Once his daughters are of marriageable age, Dua Mama hosts a big party attended by the best of the Indian American society. Riya wants to ensnare millionaire, Prashant Roy, and Amara watches them spend the evening together. But Prashant's mother, Mrs. Roy, wants a traditional girl for her son, and – to everyone's surprise – chooses Amara.

Chapter 7: Three weeks later Amara and Prashant are married. Biji is thrilled as she feels their American Dream has finally come true. She ignores the cold vibes from Dua Mama and his family. During the wedding Amara worries over Prashant's detachment and the small details that go wrong, but she tells everyone that the wedding was perfect.

Chapter 8: Amara spends her wedding night feeling shy and fearful, but Prashant goes off to sleep instantly. He takes Amara to dinner with his boss the next day and becomes angry at her bumpkin-like conduct. Amara's marriage takes an unexpected turn as she realizes that Prashant is turned off by her traditional way of thinking, and doesn't take to her or marriage.

Chapter 9: Over five years, Amara tries to 'Americanize' herself, by wearing dresses instead of saris, Jimmy Choo's instead of Bata, and mascara instead of sindoor. But Prashant continues to ignore her, staying out of the house sometimes for whole nights, either working or playing golf. Since he doesn't allow Amara to work, she spends her time alone at home thinking about their marriage and her husband. Amara wants to have children, but Prashant refuses.

Chapter 10: Prashant tells Amara that his mother is coming to live with them for an indefinite time. Fortunately, Amara gets along with dominating Mrs. Roy. Even Amara's relationship with Prashant improves when he sees how much effort she is making with his mother. Mrs. Roy promises Amara that she will speak to Prashant about their marriage, but just as Amara feels hopeful, Mrs. Roy passes away.

Chapter 11: After Prashant's mother dies he tells Amara that he married her as per his mother's wishes, and has never loved her. He asks her for a divorce, and gives her six months to move out. Then he vanishes from the house, and tells Biji and Baba to look after a 'sick' Amara, since he has to be 'out-of-town for work'. Amara finds that her parents are enjoying respect and popularity within the Indian American society. Even Baba finally likes living in America. Therefore, she is unable to tell them about her problems with Prashant.

Chapter 12: Amara visits Stacy and tells her about her impending divorce. Stacy advises her to talk to Prashant. Amara heads toward his office, but on the way she sees him with Riya, and assumes they're seeing each other. Still, Amara tries to change Prashant's mind. Prashant tells her that his love for Riya is unreciprocated, and adds that he still wants a divorce.

Chapter 13: Amara goes to live with her parent's but is unable to tell them of her separation. They realize something is wrong as they are being treated with a sudden coldness by Indian Americans. Then Baba and Biji find Amara's divorce papers. In the conservative Indian American society, a divorced woman is shunned, so on learning the truth her disappointed and angry parents throw Amara out of their house.

Chapter 14: Riya, married with children, has a change of heart and takes Amara in, helping her pick up the practical pieces of her life together. A month later, when Biji is hospitalized for a concussion, Amara finds out that her parents have been ousted by the Indian American society and plan to return to India. She insists on coming to India with them. They agree on the condition that she doesn't speak of her divorce to anyone, warning her that the Indian society would be crueler to her than the Indian American society.

Chapter 15: The Malhotra family returns to India after seventeen years, and are surprised at India's progress and modernity. Baba and Biji begin to enjoy success and comforts, but refuse to talk to Amara. Amara is still wallowing in self-doubt, when Biji walks into her room telling her that she plans to keep Amara locked in her room.

Chapter 16: On hearing Biji's threat, Amara leaves the house and goes for a walk, where she discovers the new Shimla. She bumps into her old neighbor and friend Shikha, who is the only divorcee Amara knew before she left India. Shikha is remarried with children, and helps Amara deal with the alienation and grief over her broken marriage.

Chapter 17: Under Shikha's guidance, Amara stops feeling guilty about being a divorcee and starts a consulting business for potential Indian immigrants, a job she was doing half-heartedly in America with Stacy. This attracts the ire of a local gang Pranna – headed by notorious politician Anirudh Sharma – that claims to protect the eroding moral fiber of India. Some Pranna men throw rocks through Amara's windows.

Chapter 18: Shikha warns Amara to get used to such attacks since she is a divorcee and not bother reporting them to the police. Shikha takes Amara to an exclusive meeting club of divorcees to share her experiences with. Here Amara meets a charismatic divorcee Lalit

Talwar, who has a voice deep and thick, like honey in a bottomless jar. Though Amara thinks she is not ready for love, Lalit and her friendship deepens over picnics, long walks and dinners, and she soon falls in love with him. During that time, Biji and Baba realize that the Indian society is not judging their family for Amara's divorce, as the Indian American society did. They start forgiving their daughter. Biji even introduces Amara to potential grooms, all of whom Amara rejects. Amara meets a pregnant girl, Kanika: a victim of domestic violence who wants to leave her husband and study in an American university. Even though Kanika is Anirudh Sharma's daughter Amara feels drawn to the girl.

Chapter 19: Since Kanika is not ready to be a mother, Amara finds a maternity clinic in Delhi where Kanika can deliver her baby, give her up for adoption and leave directly for America. Lalit, Shikha and she take Kanika to Delhi to visit a doctor. Unfortunately, Anirudh Sharma catches them, attacks their homes and locks Kanika away.

After you've written the synopsis, you must get down to writing your book. Begin by nailing the opening and closing chapter. How does that work? Let's begin at the beginning.

Ideally, your chapters must be in the range from 2000 to 3000 words.

You can if you wish deviate from linear narratives. For example, Amitava Kumar's *The Lovers* was described in the blurb as "a decidedly modern novel that blends story and reportage, anecdote and annotation, picture and text, fragment and essay". These elements were present in the book with academic papers, handwritten notes, photographs of elephants, screenshots of films like Dr Kotnis, and Picasso's drawings. Avant-garde, right?

But, if you're writing fiction, however modern, don't forget a little thing called a story, that's what people will read it for over your technique, however impressive.

The way a story begins is important. It must strike a chord in the reader. If you nail that first line, that first paragraph and the first page, you immediately win the loyalty and respect of your reader. You catch their attention. You compel them to turn the page and read the rest of your story.

An opening line should be arresting, like some of the most famous ones in novels and non-fiction:

> Happy families are all alike; every unhappy family is unhappy in its own way.
>
> — *Leo Tolstoy, Anna Karenina*

> We are going to die, and that makes us the lucky ones.
>
> — *Richard Dawkins, Unweaving The Rainbow*

Now that you've nailed the structure of your book, the beginning and the middle (thanks to the synopsis), don't rush through its ending, a common mistake among new writers. Imagine what a reader feels like when she's invested herself in the book, but is left with a rushed, muddled and unsatisfactory ending. It's like capping a gourmet meal with soggy pie. Close with beautiful words. Give the reader that feeling of leaving home. This is what will stay with her as she puts your book away. Aim for that reaction.

Read these beautiful closing lines in fiction and poetry.

> In my swimsuit, I stand on the side and raise my arms and then leap into that deep-blue water.
>
> — *Sachin Kundalkar, Cobalt Blue*

> They are lifted higher and higher by air currents as they wheel and arc and sail towards the last hill of the world.
>
> — *Anuradha Roy, The Folded Earth*

It matters not how strait the gate,
How charged with punishments the scroll,
I am the master of my fate,
I am the captain of my soul.

— *William Ernest Henley, Invictus*

A good ending is to a book what good dessert is to a meal, the perfect finish.

The Perfect Book Title

YOUR BOOK will initially be judged by its title so choose it carefully. The title must befit the tone of your book. It must convey the theme of the book. It must draw the attention of the reader. It also needs to give the reader a sense of where in the market it fits. Does it sound like commercial fiction or literary fiction, is it pop science or academic? It has to achieve that fine balance of inhabiting the appropriate genre for it while still sounding original and memorable. If you title your book *Bleak House*, the reader will know it probably isn't chick-lit, and if you call it *The Jadoo Of Your Love*, they'll know it probably isn't literary fiction.

Selecting the right title is a difficult process. If you're out of ideas use this simple trick: take a piece of paper and write down all the words that come to your mind when you think of your book. Move these words around—put them together, rip them apart, think of random permutations and combinations—till you hit upon a few options that make for a good title. Keep your ears and eyes open for words that sound good together, and do justice to your book. String together captivating phrases, peculiar sentences, or striking words. Select one main title that you pitch your book with, but keep at least four to five other options ready in case your publisher or you wish to change the title at a later stage.

These are some of the books have had me at the title: *The God Of Small Things*; *English, August*; *The Inheritance Of Loss*;

47

Unaccustomed Earth; The Palace Of Illusions; Maximum City: Bombay Lost And Found; Chronicles Of A Corpse Bearer; The Difficulty Of Being Good; A Bad Character; Erotic Stories For Punjabi Widows; Maps For Lost Lovers; A God In Every Stone; How To Get Filthy Rich In Rising Asia; A Case Of Exploding Mangoes; The Illicit Happiness Of Other People; Hullabaloo In The Guava Orchard; The Curious Incident Of The Dog In The Night-Time; Women Who Run With The Wolves; Hot, Flat, And Crowded; How Stella Got Her Groove Back; To Kill A Mockingbird; Gone With The Wind; One Hundred Years Of Solitude; The Grapes Of Wrath; The Hitchhiker's Guide To The Galaxy; Love In The Time Of Cholera; The Old Man And The Sea; A Tale Of Two Cities; Island Of A Thousand Mirrors; White Teeth; Kafka On The Shore; Utterly Monkey; and *Half Of A Yellow Sun.*

In non-fiction, I love these titles: *The Sex Lives Of Cannibals; Mothering A Muslim; Getting Stoned With Savages; How I Became A Tree; How To Win Friends And Influence People; The Five People You Meet In Heaven; What To Expect When You're Expecting; Lunch With A Bigot; A Day In The Life Of America, The Subtle Art Of Not Giving A F*ck,* And *Our Moon Has Blood Clots.*

Good titles make good books. Choose yours carefully.

PART THREE:
How To Be A Writer

You As A Writer

AS YOU get ready to bring to the front vivid and colorful shades of the inner world of human feelings and sensibilities, see if you are prepared to be a writer:

Ask Yourself Why – Before you begin your journey as a writer, ask yourself why you want to write. If you're writing only to become famous, or to win awards, or to make lakhs with a bestseller, you'll likely end up disappointed. Don't romanticise writing or being published. It is the toughest thing you'll ever do. Writing is a soul-wrenching all-consuming process that will demand that you put the rest of your life on hold. Write because you love writing. Write without expecting anything in return. Your ultimate reward will come in the smell of a new book, your new book, which will contain years of your life, your dreams of sending your book on its own journey, out into the world, hoping it's accepted with a gracious heart and mind. That is happiness. Nothing, no one, no award, no fame, can ever replicate that feeling of joy.

Be Authentic – Don't write in a genre that's currently selling if you don't know the first thing about it. Don't strive to be someone else or ride the popularity wave. Don't pre-determine your writing by peripheral factors; no city, no race, no gender, no religion, no amount of recognition or appreciation should frame your work. Your stories should be formed and developed keeping only the moments in mind, those epiphanic moments when the character or the plot or the truth, or all of the above, reveal themselves, most often without even knowing it, and it all comes together or falls apart. Exactly like life. Write what comes to you. Write the story that comes to you. Be real. Don't hit a false note.

Cherish Words – This doesn't mean that you mug-up a dictionary. It means that as a writer you must love words, new words, old words, hackneyed words, bad words. Play scrabble, do crossword puzzles, highlight every word that you don't know. Discover a new word every single day. My favourite word is 'Panglossian'. I love the roll of this word on my tongue and the meaning it evokes: a state of happiness. What's yours?

Go On A Journey – It's a curious thing, this whole writing business. You have to be disengaged, but highly involved; you have to have wherewithal but retain a childlike gung-ho-ness; you have to be an observer but you have to actively participate. Prepare yourself to tap into your introvert and extrovert side. Don't stick to the familiar. Do not be afraid. Break every rule. Ask questions. Seek answers. Remember, writing a book is like jumping off a cliff without knowing where you'll land, or whether you'll land at all. Stay the courage, my friend.

Be A Storyteller And A Writer – A storyteller must possess sensitivity, empathy, and social intelligence. This is inherent to someone's personality or experience. But writing is a craft. A writer must be able to write as well as say a Salman Rushdie. This is a talent that can be acquired through discipline and developed with practice. If you can perfect both skills, then when inspiration strikes or that perfect story comes your way, you'll know exactly what to do with it.

Create Time And Space – While writing his wondrous *The Blind Man's Garden*, Pakistani author Nadeem Aslam did not meet a single person for 16 months! Like most writers Aslam is a fascist when it comes to his 'writing time'. Set your own writing time. Set your space and pace. Find what works for you as a person and according to your lifestyle. I find that I cannot keep rigid hours. I am more creative and efficient without a set routine. So, I set myself a target at the beginning of every month ... say, in February, I'll write three chapters of my novel, or one short story, or I'll edit my new book. I use this as a looming deadline over my head. No matter how extenuating my personal circumstances, I never miss these targets. There are some days I'll do nothing but tweet, or play with my infant daughter, or read, and then there are days where I'll write without pausing for anything but air and chocolate, not in that order. Things typically average out. So, instead of writing 500 words a day like clockwork, I'll end up writing 15,000 words (and typically more) in a month. It might take you a month to write a book, or it may take you ten years. It's your book; take your time to write it. If you have a full-time job and/or children, then you'll have to likely set a schedule and stick to it. Find a window when you can write i.e. during the weekends or while commuting. Dedicate fixed hours of your day, if you can, to write and edit. Figure out what time of the day your creative juices most flow. Some writers are at their best early morning, while some like to work through the night. Set up a workspace: your favourite place to write. I am a horizontal writer who is most productive while lying down in bed, with a blanket on top of me, the bedroom door shut, and the fan off (even in the heat of May, if you can believe that). I wouldn't recommend this method. Be smart; get an ergonomic chair and table instead.

Embrace Being Alone – As Vikram Seth wrote in *A Suitable Boy*, "God save us from people who mean well." Remember, writing is done best when you're alone, so the fewer distractions you create in your real life, the better your writing life will be. Since it may not be practical to run off to a remote corner of the world and write your book in silence, learn how to write alongside your daily life, as most authors do. Everyone in your family must respect your writing time and space. Be rigid about this. Keep your mind strong and still. Learn to be alone. Learn to enjoy your own company. Remember, being alone is not the same thing as being lonely. But being lonely is something that will happen if you're a writer. When I'm writing I often feel like Miss Havisham. But I embrace this feeling. It makes me productive. And when I'm finished with a book, I find that nothing outside has really changed. A writer cannot suffer from FOMO (fear of missing out). The world will not stop moving without you. Don't forget that.

Use Social Media Smartly – Wi-Fi, WhatsApp, Twitter, Facebook and Instagram can be your worst enemies or your best friends. While actually writing, don't worry about not being hyper active on social media: the tweets, the outrage, the followers, the videos and the jokes will continue, with or without you. Put your phone on silent; turn off the notifications of WhatsApp, Facebook, Twitter and SMS. Keep the Wi-Fi off during your writing time. Fix time slots during which you'll use social media. Say, ten minutes at 9 am, 1 pm and 5 pm respectively. No more than that. When you're promoting your book however, it's a different story, but we'll get to that in a bit.

Keep Ego Away From The Artist – There exists no perfect writer. Even the greatest writers face criticism, backlash and even hatred. As a creator you have to be open to criticism. Allow your editor and your trusted friends to be brutally honest in their feedback. Criticism from them will be better than flak from a reviewer. You must listen to every criticism, however personal, however biased, and see if you can take something away from it, though there is no advice you are obliged to follow. Complacency is the death of an artist. As Rumi said, "If you are irritated by every rub, how will your mirror be polished?"

Respect Your Reader – Your reader is intelligent. Don't try to shortchange her with bad writing or bad grammar. Don't spoon-feed your reader either. Don't spell out each and everything. Let them experience your book.

Write Bad Stories – But don't publish them! The only way to become a good writer is to start out by writing bad stories. Persevere, edit, persevere, edit.

Remain Humble – Becoming competent or famous as a writer should not give you bravura or bluster, it will be your undoing. Acclaim is good, it will keep you motivated on bleak empty days, but when you're sitting alone, staring at an empty page with which to fill your thoughts, your only real motivation is your perseverance. The other important function of humility is that it prepares you for the possibility of failure and you should always be prepared to fail. Keep your ears to the ground. Listen more than you talk. It is in the silence between conversations where your stories lie. If you talk about writing in reverence and with a little insecurity, hold on to that feeling.

Don't Envy Others – Don't envy published authors, they've been where you are. What you see of authors in magazines, on podiums, at literature festivals, is just the tip of the iceberg. It's the only time the author has her moment in the sun after living most of the year in a cave—a dark, unlit, lonely cave. Don't romanticize the life of a writer, especially if you are one.

Be Prepared To Work Hard – Most renowned authors have written their books alongside full-time jobs, new babies, dwindling savings and neglected spouses. Many sacrifices and years of struggle are required to write, publish and market a book. Dedication is key.

Use Your Life As Inspiration – I never write about myself, I don't dare for fear of what that might reveal to me about myself. Yet, every story is a vicarious release of something inside me, something that unfurls and makes me lighter. A writer is inevitably a navel-gazer. While you may think your life is mundane, it's unique to the outside world. The world is looking for alterity within sameness. So draw from your own life. Write what you know best, in the style that comes most naturally to you. This way you'll write so realistically, that your reader will begin to believe that your characters actually exist. Don't forget to change real names though!

Use Your Imagination – "Look here's a table covered with a red cloth. On it is a cage the size of a small fish aquarium. In the cage is a white rabbit with a pink nose and pink-rimmed eyes. In its front paws is a carrot-stub upon which it is contentedly munching. On its back, clearly marked in blue ink, is the numeral 8." This is what Stephen King wrote in his book, *On Writing*, while demonstrating how to use your imagination. What a vivid image he's created. Do the same. Tap into yourself. Remember that episode in *Black Mirror* where an insurance adjuster uses the smell of beer to evoke a particular memory in people's minds? Use your senses to bring your most beautiful memories to paper.

Capture The Idea

Half of our writing battle is won if we learn how to immediately transcribe and restore our thoughts. When an amazing idea comes to you ... in the middle of the night, while watching a movie, or when you're out for a run you're convinced that you'll never forget it. Cut to 24 hours later and the noise of life—the WhatsApp ping, the doorbell, the baby, the *sabziwallah*, the new show on Netflix, the meaningless socialising—has taken over. These noises become the eternal sunshine on your spotless mind, your memory-eraser sticks. The idea that seemed so unforgettable, so urgent, so immediate, so beautiful at that moment is now forgotten. You'll waste hours trying to remember and it will not come back to you. Frustrating right? We've all been there. So, if you have an idea for a story, a character, a phrase—at a traffic jam, during your dreams, in the middle of sex—jot it down immediately on your laptop, notebook, or your phone. Capture your memory before it becomes one for you. An idea is elusive. A note is not. Become a memory keeper for your characters, a diary for their stories. This is called a writer's discipline and without it even the most talented storyteller cannot become a published author.

Deal With Writer's Block

IMAGINE WAKING up one day and simply freezing in front of an empty page. Writer's block is a writer's biggest nightmare. Many writers go hours and days and months without being able to write a single word. Some are filled with such self-doubt that they quit writing for good.

Don't let writer's block derail your career or your confidence as a writer. Use the following techniques to help you through:

The First Draft Is Not The Final Draft – Remember that you cannot judge yourself or your writing from your first draft. Writers don't sell books on the first draft. The first draft is for you to put down your ideas on paper. View it as almost as a diary, not a manuscript. You have plenty of time to edit, review and polish your manuscript before anyone reads it. Chill.

Get Organised – Behind every successful book is a whole lot of clutter. Every author's computer is filled with an unnumbered amount of folders that contain research papers, book ideas, half-written stories, unfinished book synopsis, stories they want to write, stories they wish they could write, tidbits that struck them as interesting from the papers. These reflect different stages of composition that sometimes grow organically into a novel, short story, poem or non-fiction, but mostly remain nothing but junk. Many authors open these folders and get lost in the deluge of data. They get overwhelmed with such excessive information.

Stop. Take a breath. If you think you need better assistance in organising your folders or your writing, you can use writing software tools like Writer's Workbench, Scrivener and Ulysses that are available for both Mac and Windows users. Scrivener has a steep learning curve but helps with plotting, outlining, organising, especially if you're self-publishing. There's also Google Docs that allows you to access your document from any location without carrying your laptop or pen drive, and it's great for team-sharing, which you may need during the edit stage of your book. Software tools like Evernote and FocusWriter are also available and free to download. Or just press delete. Think of it as Diwali cleaning, where you throw out anything you can't use.

Microsoft Word is, of course, still the most popular choice for writers, used by millions around the world, and it is simple to use. It's what I use. I've written two novels, dozens of short stories and hundreds of articles on it, without facing any major problems, except random shutdowns and unsaved documents.

Tools are a writer's best friends, whether it was the yesteryear typewriter, the pen, the laptop and now the software. See what works for you. In the end if you really want to write, your tools don't matter, your intentions do.

Set A Timetable – Most new writers do very well by setting themselves a target of 500 words a day, no matter what. This means that you'll have 60,000 words in 4 months, enough to be in sight of the end of your first draft.

Don't Compare Yourself To Others – Do you get jealous of that writer who publishes one book each year, when you can barely finish one book in ten years? Don't. It doesn't matter if you fly economy or business; you'll reach the same destination as everyone else on the plane. Don't let someone else's timeline define the timeline of your life. Relax.

Be Part Of A Support Group – Instead of competing with other writers, who are most likely in the same boat as you, form a group of writer friends who can help each other. You can decide the objective of the group: to provide feedback, to provide emotional support (a personal cheerleading squad needed during periods of existential crisis), to share resources, to set deadlines (like say, 500 words a day where you send your daily word count to each other), or all of the above. Trust me, no one empathises with a writer's angst as much as a fellow writer. If you want to do your best, then help others do their best. It will keep you focussed, disciplined and—most importantly—happy.

Give Yourself A Break – Artists are, more often than not, our own worst critics. History is witness to the fact that there is no perfect book, no perfect writer and certainly no perfect human being. Don't be over-critical of yourself or your work. Whatever you're writing, you're doing your best. And that's all that matters. Cut yourself some slack.

Take A Break – If you feel yourself burning out or uninspired, put the manuscript aside. Remove it from your mind. Focus on something else. Personally, I banish writers' weariness by throwing myself back into life. Do what works for you. Binge watch a show on Netflix. Learn how to make salsa, or GO do it! Go white water rafting to Rishikesh. Sing Kishore Kumar songs to your partner. Don't force art. Leave it to its fate. Every book and every idea has its own journey. It will come to you when the time is right.

Travel – To be able to sit down and write about the world, it's crucial to first stand up and see what's out there. It doesn't matter if you cannot afford a ticket to travel around the world. Walk around the city or town in which you live. Discover it like a new lover. Memorise every nook and cranny, every square and circle, every blotch and shimmer. Or, sit still. Enter your mind. Bring back memories of things forgotten...a moment, a smile, the smell of jasmine, your grandmother's hand stroking your head, a long stairway. Jot these down in a notebook. Use these images when you write.

Read – Immerse yourself in a book, or many, preferably in your genre.

Dispel Page Fright – Every writer sneaks up to an empty page differently. Some plan, some plunge. Some do a bit of both. Figure out what works for you. If you spend a day without getting one proper sentence down, it's okay. A writer's flow has its own troughs and ebbs.

Fuel Your Imagination – My imagination is at its most vivid when I talk to myself. While many may subscribe this habit to an insane person, I prefer to embrace it as the virtue of a creative person. I know this because good writing is the hardest form of thinking. It involves the agony of turning profoundly difficult thoughts into lucid form. And—from the time I began writing, almost twenty years ago—this lucidity has come to me when I'm at my most mundane: driving, cooking, cleaning or taking a shower. That's when I engage in a dialogue with my protagonists, my plots and my phrases. Figure out what gets your creative juices flowing, no matter how insane or offbeat it sounds to anyone else, and go with it. Start with something simple like keeping a journal and writing down your observations of a day. Think of it as a camera.

If, despite all your efforts, you're still unable to write, let it go. You're not the first writer facing writer's block and you will not be the last. Writing a book is hard work. Something's got to give. Sometimes it's you. The key is to remember that every writer who faced a block went on to write and publish books. It will happen for you when it's supposed to. Relax.

Handle Your Finances

THERE'S ONE question that every aspiring writer asks me: "Can I quit my job to become a full-time writer?" My answer is a resounding NO.

Let me explain why. In India only around 3-4% of writers sell more than 10,000 copies of their books. Yes, in a country of 1.3 billion people, 10,000 books are difficult to sell! Around 77% of authors make less than Rs 50,000 a year. Only about 2% of writers actually make a living out of writing. Even our country's bestselling authors have alternate sources of income (speaking engagements, family businesses, corporate jobs, TV shows, scriptwriting, movie deals) as, sadly, there is little money to be made by writing books.

If you hear other new writers boasting about getting fat advances or writing bestsellers, treat this with a pinch of salt. In our country people project success or happiness, whether in its possession or not. The reality is very different.

A writer has to buy herself a laptop, drink coffee, guzzle alcohol, eat stress snacks, and pay electricity bills that are huge due to all that late night writing. But your muse does not care for such bourgeois matters. She comes and goes as she pleases, leaving you—the writer—a starving, or at least, struggling artist. For your book advance and royalties will help you pay one or two month's rent, if you're lucky.

Most people write books out of passion, and not to make money, for writing does nothing for your bank balance. Only the top few bestselling authors in India make enough money to write full-time. Personally, I dipped into my savings made over ten years at a regular job to afford a year off to write my third novel. The year became many as I found a way to pay my bills by freelance writing and journalism. But it took the success of two prior books for me to take such a risk.

Unless you were born to an inheritance or happened to have won a lottery, build a secure financial foundation before taking up writing full-time. Some of the best authors have written their books while holding full-time jobs. They've stolen time from sleep, from family, from social engagements, from commuting, from dreary meetings, and from weekends to write. Sitting at home does not guarantee good writing. Therefore, I'd advise debut authors to keep their full-time job and continue writing. Your aim must be to get a reputed publisher, and not get caught up with how much money you can make, because there's virtually none.

That said, real writing, that raw savage beast you walk with, comes with the axe of insecurity, of a little madness, hanging above your head. So if writing consumes you and it's all you see yourself doing, then let no desk job distract you. Go where your heart takes you, just don't lose your pockets in the process.

The Importance Of Writing Workshops

THE ART of creative writing can neither be taught nor learned. Every aspiring writer must remember that writing is a solitary pursuit and that good writing—if you have the talent—can be developed only with discipline, perseverance and a lot of tenacity. A good writing workshop, like a self-help book, will guide you in your literary pursuit, but it can help you only to a certain extent. It cannot help you write a book. It cannot help you finish writing a book. It cannot teach you how to write, or how to find your voice or story. So, while writing workshops are helpful for writers wanting to publish a piece of fiction or non-fiction, the real benefit is to escalate this learning to become a 'better' writer.

In my late 20's, when I was living in New York, I attended many writing workshops and found them to be immensely helpful in my trajectory as a writer. These workshops forced me to write within a strict deadline and get used to critical feedback, which are essential tools if you want to grow as a writer. They helped me finish my first two books: *One & A Half Wife* and *Happy Birthday*. When I returned to India in 2013, I found that there were scarcely any writing workshops despite the fact that almost everyone I met wanted to be a writer! This is a pity and I'm sure many of you aspiring writers are struggling due to this. To help you, I've compiled a list of regular writing classes and workshops, as well as some distant and online writing courses that you can take. Do crosscheck these on Google before you apply. There are many occasional writing workshops that crop up, especially in centres of art and culture, so keep a lookout. Good luck!

Writing Workshops
The Xavier Institute of Communications (XIC) – Mumbai
The British Council – Delhi and Kolkata
The Jawaharlal Nehru University (JNU) – Delhi
Bharatiya Vidya Bhavan – Delhi
Distance Writing Courses
Symbiosis – Pune
IGNOU – Indira Gandhi
Online Writing Courses
Winghill Writing School
The Writer's Workshop
Quality of Course
The Writers Bureau
Coursera
The Writers' Market (Information)
New York City Writing Courses
Gotham Writing Workshop
Sackett Street
YMCA Writer's Voice
The New School
The BBC

CHAPTER TWO
PUBLISHING

If the real world were a book, it would never find a publisher. Overlong, detailed to the point of distraction and ultimately, without a major resolution.

— *Jasper Fforde*

Introduction To Indian Publishing

BEFORE WE get deep into this chapter, let's take a quick look at some statistics. According to the *India Book Market Report (2016)*, India is the sixth largest publisher in the world and the second largest publisher in the world for English-language books. That's huge! Led by educational books, publishing is a $6.76 billion sector expected to grow at an astounding 19.3% until 2020 (Nielsen Report, 2016). There are over 9000 publishers publishing around one-lakh books every year. This means that almost 250 books are published every day in India. 55% sales are of English books, 35% of Hindi books, and the rest of regional language books. 65% of English-language book sales come from Maharashtra, Tamil Nadu, Andhra Pradesh and Kerala. All these make us the world's third-largest English books market, according to the *International Publishers Association*. This is despite the fact that sales are measured in only a selection of bookshops and excludes some online retailers, notably Amazon.

We are also the third largest readers for English books in the world. Contrary to popular perception, on average, Indians spend more time reading than any of their counterparts around the world, according to the World Culture Score Index. This is about 10.5 hours every week, as compared to say the Americans who spend 5.5 hours per week reading.

According to an article in the *Financial Times* (www. ft.com/content/32dbf05e-a7c9-11e4-8e78-00144feab7de), book sales in mature economies such as Britain and America have stagnated; in India, by contrast, the market has grown 41 per cent since 2011, with 18 million copies sold in English and local languages in 2015, according to data from the Nielsen BookScan. Literacy in India is rising rapidly, from 65% in 2001 to 74% in 2011, and it is predicted to reach 90% in 2020. This can only mean more readers vying to buy more books.

Sounds promising, right? Now, the reality check. The publishing industry is deeply fragmented, distribution is disorganized, and piracy is rampant. On top of that—proving my point that almost everyone wants to be a writer—an average publisher receives around 40-60 manuscripts a day. This means around 300 manuscripts per week and 1200 manuscripts per month. The chances of your book being picked out of this slush pile are pretty slim, only about 10% to 5%. Yes, almost 90-95% of all manuscripts that get sent to publishing houses are rejected. Ouch!

Back in 2011, when I finished writing my first novel, *One & A Half Wife*, I did not know that my journey as a writer had just begun. As it is, writing is a soul-wrenching all-consuming process that demands you to put the rest of your life on hold. Yet, writing plays a small part in getting published, because the hardest part of being a debut author is to find a publisher. It's difficult to make a breakthrough, but it's not impossible, since publishers (especially the local ones) are on the lookout for new voices and are willing to give debut writers a chance. So, give it your best shot! Find out how your book can make the cut!

How To Write A Synopsis

THE FIRST step in publishing your book is to write a synopsis. Simply put, the synopsis is an outline of your book. It is what happens in your book from the beginning to the end. It's your story's narrative arc and your non-fiction book's central premise. Some authors make outlines before they begin writing their book, some don't. But almost all publishing houses and agents require a synopsis, so you will have to write one at some point. If you've already written a synopsis (see *Chapter One: How To Structure Your Book*), you can use that to send to a publisher. If you haven't, you'll need to write one at this stage.

If you think that writing an 80,000-word book is tough, try summarizing it in 1000 words or less. Here are some tips. First, keep the synopsis brief and easy to follow (1-4 pages is best). A typical synopsis will be around 1000 words or 3 pages. For a short-story collection, you will have to summarise each story in 2-4 sentences. Second, reveal the ending of your book. An agent or publisher is not going to appreciate it if you leave them hanging or use rhetorical questions to summarise your book. This synopsis will not come on your book cover or on the book's Amazon page, so there is no need for suspense. Keep it simple and straightforward. Thirdly, write the synopsis in the present tense, using the same text format as you did for your manuscript (see *Chapter One: Format Your Manuscript*). For fiction, you can put character names in caps for ease of reading. Fourthly, the synopsis does not have to cover every supporting character and tertiary plot point. The editor or agent wants to understand who your central characters are, what their main conflict is, and how they resolve it. A quick tip here: if your ending does not make sense without the mention of a particular character or plot point, then use them in the synopsis. For non-fiction, editors want to get an idea of your proposal, so send them the synopsis accordingly. Lastly, don't make your synopsis dull and sterile. The character's feelings or the scene's mood has to be conveyed, as and when important. In non-fiction, the editor wants to get a sense of your writing style, so don't slack off.

To give you an idea, I've written two kinds of synopsis for my novel *One & A Half Wife*. The first is a standard one-paragraph synopsis, something like an elevator pitch of your book. It is something you must write and perhaps memorise so that when people (note: editors) ask you what your book is about, you don't fumble. You can use this in your query letter as well. The second is a 3-page synopsis that some publishing houses or agents ask for. As before, I've removed the spoilers, in case you intend to read the novel. If you've written your book's chapter-by-chapter synopsis (see *Chapter One: How To Structure Your Book*), use that as reference.

SAMPLE OF A ONE-PARAGRAPH SYNOPSIS:

ONE-AND-A-HALF WIFE tells the story of Amara Malhotra who—unlike other Indian immigrants in America—is not destined to achieve the American Dream. Much to the anxiety of her overwrought mother, Biji, and her stoical father, Baba, Amara leads an uninspiring life, till the time she marries millionaire Prashant Roy. When her marriage fails and the Indian American community ostracizes her, Amara decides to return to her hometown Shimla after seventeen years. Amara comes to present-day India, which is fumbling with its growing modernity, and in this schizophrenic atmosphere she bridges the chasm within herself to discover what she wants from life.

SAMPLE OF A THREE-PAGE SYNOPSIS:

AMARA MALHOTRA is born on a torrential July evening in Shimla to a domineering mother, BIJI, who wants two things but asks for three, and a stoical lawyer father, BABA, who works like a Chief Justice and earns like a peon. In celebration of her much-awaited birth, Biji throws Amara off a sacred fifty-foot temple tower, so she comes out healthy and strong and lucky, like a melodious jingle. Her rich uncle, DUA MAMA, hears that Amara survives and assuming that her valor foretells a great destiny, he applies for her family's Green Card to America. Amara grows up being told that getting married, listening to her mother, and achieving the American Dream is all she must desire from life.

Fourteen years pass. When the Green Cards fail to arrive on time, Biji consults Shimla's most famous parrot astrologer. Much to Biji's chagrin the astrologer predicts that the Green Cards will come, but Amara's marriage will fail. He secretly gives Amara an emerald stone as keepsake. Soon the Green Cards arrive and the Malhotra family prepares to leave for America. They reach America to start a middle-class life in Edison, New Jersey, under the shadow of Dua Mama and his beautiful snooty daughter, RIYA. Amara attends high school but feels lost among the sophisticated students, a cute boy with straw legs named Bob, and the American accent she cannot follow. She doesn't want to disappoint Baba and Biji – who have pinned their American Dream on her – so she makes a plan to befriend Riya. Biji insists Riya will help Amara meet eligible Indian boys. Amara goes to school wearing Riya's discarded clothes and homemade makeup, but Riya makes fun of her, in front of Bob.

Humiliated, Amara turns her attention to studies and eventually attends a state university. In college she grows out of Riya's shadow and befriends STACY LONG, her vivacious accounting classmate who wants to be anything but an accountant, and who introduces Amara to McDonald's and boyfriends. After college Amara's parents want her to continue living with them, so Amara starts working at Dua Mama's accounting firm.

Once his daughters are of marriageable age, Dua Mama hosts a party attended by the best of Indian Americans. Riya wants to ensnare millionaire, PRASHANT ROY, but his mother wants a traditional girl, and – to everyone's surprise – chooses Amara. Three weeks later Amara and Prashant get married. Biji feels that their American Dream has finally come true and enjoys her new popularity in the Indian American community. But Prashant is turned off by Amara's traditional way of thinking, and does not take to Amara or marriage. Over five years, Amara tries to 'Americanize' herself, by wearing dresses instead of saris, Jimmy Choo's instead of Bata, and mascara instead of sindoor. But Prashant remains aloof, even refusing to start a family that Amara so desires. After Prashant's mother dies, he tells Amara that he married her as per his mother's wishes, but does not love her. Prashant asks Amara for a divorce. Amara tries to change his mind but relents when she finds out that he loves Riya, though it is unreciprocated.

Amara goes to live with her parent's but is unable to tell them of her separation. On learning the truth her disappointed and angry parents throw Amara out of their house. With nowhere to go, Amara bumps into Riya. Riya, married with children, has a change of heart and takes Amara in, helping her pick up the broken pieces of her life. Amara learns that due to her divorce, the Indian American society is ostracizing her family. Unable to bear the brand of failed immigrants, Baba and Biji decide to return to India after seventeen years; Amara insists on coming with them.

The Malhotra family comes to present-day to India and is surprised at its progress and modernity. Baba and Biji begin to enjoy the success and comforts they missed in America. Amara, still wallowing in self-doubt, meets her old neighbor, SHIKHA ARORA, who is the only divorcee Amara knows. Shikha, remarried with children, helps Amara deal with the grief and alienation over her broken marriage. Amara starts a consulting business with Stacy. This attracts the ire of a local gang Pranna – headed by notorious politician ANIRUDH SHARMA – that claims to protect the eroding moral fiber of India. Shikha advises Amara to ignore Pranna and takes her to a meeting club of divorcees, where she can share her experiences. Here Amara meets charismatic divorcee LALIT TALWAR, who has a voice deep and thick, like honey in a bottomless jar. Though Amara is not ready for love, she can't resist Lalit and their attraction deepens over picnics, long walks and dinners.

During that time, Biji and Baba realize that the Indian society is not judging their family for Amara's divorce, as the Indian American society did. They start forgiving their daughter. Biji even introduces Amara to potential grooms, all of whom Amara rejects.

Soon Amara meets a pregnant girl, KANIKA SHARMA, a victim of domestic violence who wants to leave her husband and study at Boston University. Amara helps Kanika even though she is Anirudh Sharma's daughter. What happens next?

How To Write A Query Letter

LEARNING HOW to write the perfect query letter is your only chance at getting an agent or publisher interested in your manuscript. Writing a good query letter is almost as important as writing a good book. In fact, some people compose such stellar query letters that they get a book deal without even writing the book! But that's obviously a risky way to go about doing things if you're an unpublished author.

So, what's a query letter? It's a one-page letter or 300-word email that you send to a publisher or agent to get them so excited about your book that they're compelled to read your submission package (*see next chapter*). Publishers receive hundreds of query letters a week, sometimes even in a day. How can you make sure that yours stands out? By writing a good query that highlights your story's USP, your writing history, and your strengths.

But first, learn how to compose a query letter:

+ Make it personalised. Address the agent or publisher by their surname so they know that you're not sending out a blanket query letter copy-pasted to every publisher (this shortcut reeks of laziness). If you've met the editor or agent, mention where and when. If you have a recommendation, mention by whom and why they think you're worth recommending.

+ Mention the title, word count and genre of your book. Use only ONE title. Do not say it's a 'tentative title'. It's always a tentative title till the book goes to print.

+ Introduce your book with a one-line hook.

+ Elaborate on the book with a one-paragraph synopsis, around four to six sentences long.

+ Introduce yourself with a bio. Mention any publishing history, writing awards, writing credentials, writing residencies and writing scholarships. Be specific with names. If you don't have any writing history don't make things up. Everything today can be found on Google. You'll be caught and blacklisted. Don't mention that you're new—it's understood by omission. Don't apologise for being a debut author—everyone starts somewhere. Mention your career only if it adds value to the book. If you're a nutritionist writing a diet book, or a CBI officer writing a spy novel, or a journalist who can leverage contacts during marketing, then your credentials help. Otherwise, don't draw attention to them.

+ If you're writing non-fiction, you must mention the target market you're writing for, why you're the most qualified person to write the book, and the readership size you expect for the book.

+ Close simply with a thank you and look forward. Sign off with a simple 'sincerely'. Mention your email, phone number (if you wish) and website (if any) in the signature.

+ No matter what you do, do not make grammatical mistakes, do not misspell the editor's or agent's name, do not call them Ms. when they're a Mr. or vice-versa (a very common and infuriating mistake), do not exceed 400 words, do not send pictures and photos or scented candles with the query, do not send an incomplete or unpolished sample manuscript. Keep it simple and straightforward.

SAMPLE QUERY LETTER TO A PUBLISHER

Dear Ms./Mr. ,

I am seeking representation for my novel ONE & A HALF WIFE (89,000 words), which was shortlisted for the *Amazon Breakthrough Novel Award*. ONE & A HALF WIFE is a coming-of-age tale that taps into the universal themes of family, love and displacement, while delineating the dwindling American Dream for Indian immigrants.

The novel tells the story of Amara Malhotra who—unlike other Indian immigrants in America—is not destined to achieve the American Dream. Much to the anxiety of her overwrought mother, Biji, and her stoical father, Baba, Amara leads an uninspiring life, till the time she marries millionaire Prashant Roy. When her marriage fails and the Indian American community ostracizes her, Amara decides to return to her hometown Shimla after seventeen years. Amara comes to present-day India, which is fumbling with its growing modernity, and in this schizophrenic atmosphere she bridges the chasm within herself to discover what she wants from life.

I am a journalist and have worked with NDTV Profit, Times Now and Bloomberg-UTV. I've attended several writing workshops in New York such as *The Sackett Street, Gotham, Winghill* and *Writer's Voice*. My non-fiction articles have appeared in publications including *Little India, The South Asian Times, MiD Day, Man's World* and *Hindustan Times*. My short stories have been published or are forthcoming in *EGO Magazine, Every Day Fiction, Six Sentences, Muse India, Pothi Magazine* and *DifferSenses*. I am currently also working on a collection of short stories and a second novel based in—and between—India and China.

Please find attached in .doc the detailed synopsis, chapter outline and the first three chapters of my novel. I would be glad to send the full manuscript for your review.

Thank you in advance for your time and consideration. I look forward to hearing from you.

Sincerely,
Meghna Pant
****

SAMPLE QUERY LETTER TO A PUBLISHER FOR NON-FICTION

Dear Ms./Mr. ,

I am an award-winning Indian author and seek your representation for my new self-help book HOW TO GET PUBLISHED IN INDIA (80,000 words).

Almost every person wants to be a writer and almost every writer wants to be a bestseller. Almost no one knows how. Publishing a book is an intimidating, frustrating and confusing endeavour. Who can thousands of aspiring writers turn to for answers?

HOW TO GET PUBLISHED IN INDIA is India's first and only comprehensive book on writing, publishing and selling a book. This one-stop resource is an essential guide to anyone who wants to get published. Packed with writing tips, marketing hacks and publishing secrets, the book touches upon every genre from literary novels to commercial fiction novels to short stories to poems to non-fiction, so there's something in this book for everyone, whether it's a novelist, a poet, a ghostwriter, a corporate leader, a romantic youngling or a literary wizard.

Apart from the how-to survival guide, the book also showcases a collection of interviews with India's most prominent authors, editors, publishers, ghost writers, poets, designers and agents—from Jeffrey Archer to Twinkle Khanna to Shobhaa De—who share their secrets, their struggles and their victories in the publishing world, with candid insights and confessions.

As an acclaimed author of several books who's attended and conducted writing workshops, I know there's a big gap in the market for a book like this. Frankly, I wish someone had written a book like this when I was starting out. Therefore, I believe the book will sell very well, especially to aspiring writers who are equal (if not more) in number to the readers in India today.

Please read the attached submission package that contains:
1. Chapter Synopsis
2. Table of Contents
3. Two Sample Chapters
4. Author Bio

If this interests you, I can send across the full manuscript and marketing proposal.

Thanks in advance for your time and consideration. I look forward to hearing from you.

Sincerely,
Meghna Pant
****

SAMPLE QUERY LETTER TO AN AGENT

Dear Ms./Mr. ,

I am an award-winning Indian author and seek your representation for my new novel MEN WITHOUT GOD (70,000 words). As you represent authors such as XXX and XXX, I think my novel might be a good fit for your list.

The year is 2022. China declares war on India. Pillage and plunder ensues. The war comes to an abrupt halt when a supernatural event saves the obscure Indian town of Lalbag from annihilation. Even as China renews its efforts to invade Lalbag, a greater calamity awaits this sleepy town. The town's richest man, and possibly the greediest, stumbles upon a dangerous secret that will destroy his family. A fierce and forbidden love between a servant and his mistress threatens to end the town's immunity. Meanwhile, an Indian man gets married to a Chinese woman, a sorceress casts deadly spells on the townspeople, and a psychic keeps turning water into blood, sending the town deeper into tragedy.

A dark tale set in—and between—China and India, MEN WITHOUT GOD is a powerful portrayal of longing, strife and family in the wake of war.

I am an award-winning author, columnist, feminist and speaker. My debut collection of short stories HAPPY BIRTHDAY (Random House) was longlisted for the Frank O'Connor International Award (2014). ONE & A HALF WIFE (Westland)—my bestselling debut novel— won the national Muse India Young Writer Award and was shortlisted for the Amazon Breakthrough Novel Award. I've also won the FON South Asia Short Story Award (2016) and The Bharat Nirman Award (2017) for my writing. My short story *Cows That Glow* was longlisted for the Commonwealth Short Story Prize (2018).

Please find attached the first thirty pages of my novel. I would be glad to send the rest of the manuscript for your review.

Thank you in advance for your time and consideration. I look forward to hearing from you.

Sincerely,
Meghna Pant
****

Get Your Submission Package Ready

THE FIRST step in getting published is to finish a polished manuscript, which translates into edit, edit and more edit. For instance, I wrote the first draft of my novel, *One & A Half Wife*, in two months, but took ten more months to edit it. After I was satisfied that my novel was ready to be sent to publishers, I spend weeks composing a synopsis of the novel to be pasted in the introductory email to publishers. I spend days thinking how to plump up my bio with the best writing credentials an unpublished author could have. I did research on publishers by going online to check their submission guidelines and preferred genre of work (i.e. some may not accept short stories). After that, I compiled a submission package for each publisher, as per their specific guidelines, which took two-three weeks, and only then started approaching them.

So, what goes into a submission package? The requirement varies, depending on the publisher, but typically it includes your query letter, synopsis, and either three sample chapters of your novel, five short stories of your short-story book, five poems of your poetry book, or your proposal in case you're submitting non-fiction. Some publishers ask only for the query letter, while others ask for the entire submission package. Again, each publisher has their own requirement so read their submission guidelines carefully before sending them anything.

First, you have to submit a standard query letter. This can be via email, or a hard copy via regular post or courier. Check the website of the publisher where this will be clearly stated. If you're sending a hard copy, make sure you retain your own copy, since your submitted copy will not be returned to you. If you think it will help you to personally visit the office of the publisher, it will not. They will either send you back, or request you to handover the submission package at the reception. They may even blacklist you. Don't take that risk.

While the good news is that most publishers accept unsolicited manuscripts, the slush pile is so deep that there's little chance of someone looking at it. Therefore, if they do, you have to catch their interest on the first page itself.

At this point, let me quickly touch upon the issue of copyright, which seems to be on every new author's mind. The copyright for your book rests with you. It's an implicit rule. So, you do not have to put a copyright sign on your sample manuscript. No, you do not have to mention that the copyright rests with you in your query letter. No, the publisher is not going to steal your idea/book/name/character name/dedication page etc. This is not the movie industry. The entire system of publishing runs on a code of honour. A writer's work is rarely, if ever, poached. So, don't make a fuss over it. You'll come across as an amateur or, worse, belligerent.

If your submission piques a publisher's interest, they may not wait for the customary three to six months to respond to you. More likely, they'll respond within a week or month. Westland responded to my submission of *One & A Half Wife* within two hours, while other publishing houses came in with their offers over the next month or two (though one responded after nine months by which time my book had already been sent to the printers!).

They will then ask you to send your full manuscript for further evaluation. This does not mean that they're publishing your manuscript; it means that they've liked what they saw in your query letter, synopsis and sample chapters. This second round of evaluation can also take weeks or months, as editors scrutinise your book for both its literary and commercial merit. Be patient. Do not hound them with follow-up emails or calls. Work on your next book. Better still, go travelling, or go out! You deserve it.

Word of caution: Finish your novel—down to the final draft—before you approach a publisher. This way, if they ask for a full manuscript, you will not come across as a bumbling unprofessional by asking them to wait for a few months while you finish writing the rest of your book. Only established authors can pitch first and finish their manuscript on commission later. For the new writer this luxury does not exist. So, when you have a foot in the door don't slam it shut. Be prepared.

If you don't hear back from a publisher, it's important to be patient and make follow-ups only after giving them their stipulated time period for review (stated on their website). Keep in mind that the trick to getting published is talent, passion, tenacity and patience, oodles and oodles of it.

If you get rejected, do not take it personally. Don't ask the publisher for a reason, they will not give you one. Do not resend the book unless you've drastically changed it, in which case you must send a fresh submission package, after a good waiting period, and by mentioning the same to the publisher.

You can send a submission package to many publishers at the same time. This is called a simultaneous submission. It will increase the probability of your book getting published, while reducing the time you spend waiting for each publisher to respond (it can take a year, in some cases!). You don't have to inform them of the same. But if one publishing house expresses interest in your book, you can use that as leverage to entice other publishers. There's nothing a publisher loves more than to sign an author who another publisher wants! Below is a sample email that you can compose if you reach that situation.

A word of caution: do not lie. Publishers know one another. You will get caught.

SAMPLE FOLLOW-UP EMAIL:

Dear Ms./Mr. ,

I had submitted the proposal of my novel ONE & A HALF WIFE for your review on 11th January 2011.

There is some good news on that front that I wanted to share with you. The novel was long-listed for the *Cinnamon Press Novel Writing Award* in the U.S. This is the second award bestowed on the novel even before its publication.

Also, I am aware of your review process, but another publishing house has expressed interest in publishing my novel. While it's heartening to receive such positive reception to my work, you remain my number one choice as a publisher. Therefore, if possible, can I request a revert regarding my submission earlier than you have currently scheduled?

I appreciate your cooperation and look forward to hearing from you.

Regards,
Meghna Pant

If you're one of the lucky few, you can watch your book go into auction!
In summary: Stick to each publisher's submission guidelines. Submit your customised submission package to each publisher. Make simultaneous submissions to increase your chances. Keep your full manuscript ready before you approach publishers. Be patient. Do not hound the publisher. Do not be dejected by rejections, as every writer goes through it. It's difficult to make a breakthrough, as publishers receive hundreds of manuscripts a week, but it's also not impossible, as Indian publishers are looking for new voices. Keep your fingers crossed. Be prepared.

Do You Need An Agent?

WHAT'S AN agent? An agent is someone who will represent your book to publishers. This means that they will critique your raw manuscript, make suggestions for edits, develop your proposal, pitch your book, get you the best deal from a publisher, auction your book if more than one publisher is interested, negotiate your advance and royalties, get your book published abroad and/or in regional languages, push your book during marketing, and collect your advance and royalties. An agent will be your introduction to the intimidating world of publishing. They will make sure that publishers give your book a chance, handhold you through complex book contracts, and—most importantly—be your agony aunt, guide and friend.

First, understand whether you need an agent. I never did. My debut novel got picked up without any publishing history, publishing contacts or personal leverage. It was a fairly straightforward albeit angst-ridden and tough process. Unlike the U.S. and other markets, 60-70% of books in India are picked up without agents, since the majority of publishers accept unsolicited manuscripts. This does not take away from the agent's significance, of course. An agent is ideal for someone who has never been published before, and for those authors who would rather focus on their writing than get caught up with the rigmarole and paperwork of getting published. An agent will guide you and fight for you, when you most need someone by your side. Agents are also abreast of the goings-on in the publishing world, unlike us isolated writers, so there's that. You will not be worse off without an agent, but you will be better off with one.

If you decide to get an agent, target a particular agent (not agency) whose work you're familiar with. That is: get an agent who represents authors whose work or career you admire, or who represents books that are similar to yours. Blindly submitting to an agent whose work you don't know is a waste of their time and yours. Do your research! Mention why you're interested in that particular agent in your query letter. Be professional.

I get asked this a lot during my writing workshops. Do you have to pay an agent? My answer is: "No!" A resounding NO. You never pay an agent. The agent will take a 15-20% commission from your advance and royalties *after* selling your book. If an agent asks you for money to read your manuscripts or represent you, as some of the even reputed ones do with unpublished authors, decline. Don't waste your money on someone who is doing their job: reading manuscripts and representing books. There are a lot of (even erstwhile) agents looking to hustle new authors who are either desperate or naïve. Caveat Emptor. Don't be desperate. Don't be naïve. There are many agents to choose from today.

Below is a list of agents and agencies, both national and international, along with their contact details (as publically available). You can Google more, and check for updates. Most of the mentioned foreign agents work with Indian publishing companies and Indian authors. Go to *Writer Beware* (www. sfwa.org/other-resources/for-authors/writer-beware/) to check whether the foreign agent you're approaching is legit or not. As always, make sure to check an agent's website and submission guidelines for updates and information before approaching them. Do not approach an agent until your manuscript is ready, your query letter is nailed, and you're meeting their submission guidelines.

1. Siyahi: www.siyahi.in
Contact person: Mita Kapur (mita.kapur@gmail.com)

2. Writer's Side: www.writersside.com
Contact person: Kaniskha Gupta (kanishka500@gmail.com)

3. Sherna Khambatta Literary Agency: www.shernakhambatta.com
Contact person: Sherna Khambatta (sherna_khambatta@yahoo.co.uk)

4. Red Ink Literary Agency: www.redinkliteraryagency.com
Contact person: Anuj Bahri (anuj.redink@gmail.com)

5. Jacaranda Literary Agency: www.jacarandalit.com
Contact person: Jayapriya Vasudevan (jay@jacaranda-press.com)

6. Purple Folio: www.purplefolio.com
Contact person: Urmila Dasgupta (purplefolio@gmail.com)

7. The Book Bakers: www.thebookbakers.blogspot.in
Contact person: Suhail Mathur (thebookbakers@gmail.com)

8. Lotus Lane Literary: www.lotuslit.com
Contact Person: Priya Doraswamy (contact@lotuslit.com)

9. SBI Impresario Pvt. Ltd: www.sbiimpresario.com
Contact person: Sorab Irani (sbi.impresario@gmail.com)

10. David Godwin Associates: www.davidgodwinassociates.com
Contact person: David Godwin (philippa@davidgodwinassociates.co.uk)

11. Aitken Alexander: www.aitkenalexander.co.uk
Contact person: Shruti Debi (submissions@aitkenalexander.co.uk)
12. Blake Friedmann: www.blakefriedmann.co.uk
Contact person: Isobel Dixon (isobel@blakefriedmann.co.uk)
13. William Morris Endeavor: www.wmeentertainment.com
Contact person: Eric Simonoff (ESimonoff@wmeentertainment.com)
14. Rogers, Coleridge & White Ltd.: www.rcwlitagency.com
Contact person: Peter Straus (matthew@rcwlitagency.com)
15. Curtis Brown: www.curtisbrown.co.uk
Contact person: Karolina Sutton (cbcsubmissions@curtisbrown.co.uk)

Identify The Right Publisher

INDIA HAS over 9000 publishers and counting. Below is a list of the top publishing companies. Before approaching them, check online for their updated submission guidelines, editor names, and preference for genre.

FICTION AND NON-FICTION
Bloomsbury Publishing India
Penguin Random House India
HarperCollins Publishers India
Westland Publications
Simon & Schuster
Juggernaut Books
Aleph Book Company
Rupa Publications
Hachette India
Roli Books
Jaico Publishing House
Zubaan Books
Speaking Tiger Books
Srishti Publishers
Tara-India Research Press
Manjul Publishing House (Amaryllis)

Pan Macmillan India
Leadstart Publishing
Fingerprint Publishing
APK Publishers
Grapevine India Publishers
Grey Oak Publishers
Orient Publishing

NON-FICTION
Dorling Kindersley
Hay House
Scholastic India
Sage Publications India
Pustak Mahal
S. Chand Publishing
Paragon Publishing
Wiley India

CHILDREN'S BOOKS OR YOUNG ADULT FICTION
Duckbill
Young Zubaan
Katha
Tara
Pratham
Tulika
Amar Chitra Katha

How To Handle Rejection

WHY AM I dedicating an entire chapter to 'rejection'? Because that's something you'll face as a writer. Even if you possess the literary genius of Salman Rushdie or the marketing prowess of Chetan Bhagat, at some point or another, in some way or the other, you'll face some form of rejection in your writing career. It's inevitable. If a publisher doesn't reject you, a reader will; if a reader doesn't, a reviewer will; and if they don't—surprise—you will. Writers are often their own worst critics. I know I am. Rejection will come to you at some point or the other. It could even be by way of a one-star review on Amazon, or by slow book sales. Rejection is omnipresent, and it's not kind. You'll have to learn how to deal with it in order to develop as a writer. In fact—don't fear rejection; if you're not getting rejected, you're not trying hard enough.

The first kind of rejection you may face is when a publisher rejects your book. Don't take it personally. 95% or more writers face rejection. A book proposal is evaluated on the basis of many aspects, from the writing to the structure, the style, the potential readership, the potential market for the content, and your book's commercial viability (yes, editors sit down with the sales team to decide which books to acquire). There may be many reasons why your manuscript is rejected and it may have absolutely nothing to do with your writing. Publishers have their own internal issues to deal with and targets to meet. Treat rejection as a learning lesson. It's best to enter this industry by developing a thick skin.

If you genuinely can't stand being rejected, and you find it chipping away at your confidence as a writer, then there's always self-publishing. Using this avenue, you can be the boss of your own book and chart your own course without any fear of rejection.

When your book comes out and it's lucky to get reviewed (in today's world, you're lucky if your book catches a reviewer's eye), there will be some uncomplimentary things written about it; without fail. Remember, that just like no two people look at a painting the same way, no two people read a book the same way. Your writing will not be everyone's cup of tea, and that's ok. It takes a rare book to have universal appeal. Read the reviews and see if you can take something out of them, something that will help you improve as a writer. Unfortunately, India has a lot of lazy 'reviewers' who have neither the experience nor wherewithal to write book reviews. Many of them simply copy-paste the flap text and pass a generic judgement on the book and/or the author. In these cases, treat the reviews as meaningless. Learn to distinguish constructive criticism from drivel. A book review with personal attacks or blanket statements is best ignored. If there is genuine criticism, say that you use the passive voice too much, or that hooks rather than plot points drive your book, then learn something from this. It will help you write an even better book the next time. As Salman Rushdie said, "Art is stronger than the censor." So is the artist.

The Bhagavad Gita says that you must do the action without thinking of its consequences… apply that to your writing as well. At the end of the day, you're writing because you love writing. Write the best book that you can, and leave it to its journey; forget what the world has to say about it.

Whenever you feel dejected, remember that Jonathan Livingston's *Seagull* was rejected 140 times. *Gone With The Wind* was rejected 38 times. Stephen King's *Carrie* was rejected 30 times, and J.K. Rowling's *Harry Potter* was rejected 12 times! Sometimes the world doesn't know a good thing.

What To Expect In A Publishing Contract

MANY UNPUBLISHED authors dream that they'll become rich and famous through their writing. While I hate to be the one to burst this bubble, it's better you feel the chill before you get the frostbite. A book—especially a debut—will most likely not fetch much money. This is something that every new author should bear in mind. I'm saying this to prepare you for how little money you'll make on something that will take a big chunk of your life.

If a publisher agrees to publish your manuscript, the next step they'll take is to send you a publishing contract. Most of these contracts are pretty standard. While almost everything in the contract is negotiable, most new authors either accept any terms and conditions (they're so grateful for being published) without even reading the contract, or they become belligerent, thus souring relationships (and a career in writing) even before it begins. Decide what strategy you want to adopt, depending on your talent and temperament.

But before that let's understand what a standard publishing contract contains. Keep in mind that these guidelines are subject to change, and individual to each publisher.

The first important thing for an author to look for in a contract is the advance. A book advance is what your publisher will pay you to acquire your manuscript. On average, a debut author gets paid Rs 30,000-40,000 (or less for poetry or short stories) as a book advance. Unless you're a *neta, abhineta,* celebrity, or Priyanka Chopra's dog, don't expect much more. The advance will be paid out in silos; for example: one-third on signing the agreement, one-third on delivery and approval of the manuscript, and one-third on publication of the book. An average first print run for a debut book is 2000 copies. This is for an author that the publisher has faith in. First print runs can be much less. So, when you hear of a big advance and imagine the author rolling in millions, don't. A big advance in publishing lingo means that the publisher is printing a huge run on the author's first print run. That's it.

On top of your advance, you'll also receive royalties from your publisher. Royalties are what an author gets paid on every book that sells. On average a new author gets a royalty of 7.5% on a paperback edition (books with a thin flexible cover that are meant for mass-market sales) and 10% on hardback copies (books with a thick cardboard cover that are more expensive and targeted for a niche market). This means that if your book is priced at Rs 300, you will get Rs 22.50 per book sold, before taxes. The payout of royalties is stipulated in the contract and is typically half-yearly. You'll have to sell 2000 copies, your entire first print run, to earn less than Rs 45,000. There are very few authors who manage even this.

Be warned that your book advance is against royalties. This means that only if the publisher recovers the sum they have paid you as an advance, will they start doling out royalties. Unless you cross your initial print run you'll never even get that royalty. In fact, most authors in India have never received a royalty cheque. On top of that, if any books are overstocked, damaged or given free to reviewers, they'll not bring you royalties.

Some authors find the royalty system opaque since the publishers *tell* the authors how many copies have sold versus *showing* them. This has been a bone of contention between many authors and publishers since there is no way of knowing how much your book has actually sold. Therefore, a few authors ask for an upfront flat fee and forgo the royalties.

That said, do not let a publisher prey on your newbie insecurities and offer you less than market rate, or worse still— as happens with smaller or unknown publishers—ask you to pay THEM. You may scoff but many new writers have asked me, in all earnestness, how much they'll have to 'pay' to get published! They seem to think that's how the system works. Unless you're self-publishing, the publisher will pay you for your book. Don't forget that.

The publisher will retain the right to produce, print, publish, translate, market, distribute and reproduce your work, and to license others to produce, print, publish, translate, market, distribute and reproduce your work in all editions, languages and forms/formats. This can be for a particular territory (say India) or even worldwide.

The publisher will also retain subsidiary rights like e-book rights, audio book rights, movie rights, television rights, merchandising rights, translation rights, book-club rights, and anthology rights of which the author will get a percentage. You will retain the right of being an author and hence creator of your work, therefore the copyright of the book (which will be purchased by the publisher) will remain in your name (remember this) in the format below:

Copyright © AUTHOR'S NAME followed by YEAR OF PUBLICATION

Your wiggle room as a first-time author is pretty less, but you can try to negotiate the advance, the royalty, the due date for delivery of the manuscript and edited proofs, the first print run (2000 being the norm), your number of free copies (20 being the norm), and your author discount to buy copies (40-50% being the norm).

If there is a bone of contention, then speak to your publisher and share your concerns. Do not sign on anything that you're not comfortable with as the obligation to deliver rests solely on you. If you're thinking of hiring a lawyer, good luck finding one. Lawyers in publishing are rare. And, they'll cost you much more than your advance. It might be better to get an experienced agent instead. If everything in the contract sits well with you, sign away, and welcome to the big bad world of publishing!

The Role Of Editors

AFTER YOUR contract is signed, your book will be assigned to an editor(s). Are you excited? Are you waiting for that magical moment when your editor presents you your polished manuscript ready to be sent to the printer? Are you booking your next vacation while the editor edits your book? Wait! Indulgent editors are ghosts of publishing past, so don't romanticize the relationship that yesteryear writers like F. Scott Fitzgerald and Ernest Hemingway shared with their editors. Today, you cannot leave your book editing entirely to editors. While the West still has many checks and balances to ensure the quality of a book, in India there are no such gatekeepers. Depending on your publisher, you may even end up publishing the same manuscript that you sent for submission! Surprised? Don't be. Editors in India, while exceptional, are not enough in number. They bring out hundreds of books each year under tight deadlines and with limited resources. They're starved of time. They're underpaid. They want to (and do) jump ship to more lucrative industries like advertising or TV or films. Therefore, the less work you leave for your editor the more quality edits you'll get.

Yet—and this is another mind-boggling aspect of book editing—a good publishing house will have a large number of editors. Each editor will be involved with different stages of your book and specialise in different types of editing. Befuddled? Let

me break it down. Below I've listed the editors you'll most likely
be assigned:

1. Acquisition Editor (aka Developmental/Structural/Content
   Editor) – These editors look at the big picture i.e. the forest but
   not the trees. They'll work with you to better the idea, outline
   and vision of your book. They'll look closely at the structure
   and argument in non-fiction, or the plot and character in fiction.

2. Line Editor – As the name suggests, these editors will go
   through every line of your book to ensure that your phrases
   are formed, your paragraphs transition, and your language is
   polished.

3. Copy Editor – These editors will focus on the copy of your
   book. They will correct your spellings, grammar, repetitive
   words, punctuation, hyphenation and capitalisation, to make
   your manuscript clean and consistent.

4. Proofreaders – These folks will provide the final eyes for your
   book before it goes into print. They will spot missed errors in
   punctuation, grammar, spacing, style or formatting etc.

5. Typesetters – They layout your book in the font in which it'll
   appear in the finished copy. The next step after editing is getting
   your book cover ready (*see next chapter*). Then your job as a
   writer is done (at least for this book)! Do be patient though—it
   will take 4-6 months after editing and cover designing for your
   book to be published!

Design The Perfect Book Cover

THINK OF *The Old Man And The Sea, Memoirs Of A Geisha, White Tiger, Lord Of The Flies, Moby Dick, Exit West, The Subtle Art Of Not Giving A F*uck, The Room, Dark Matter, The Luminaries, A Fine Balance, The Windfall.* What do they have in common? Yes, a good cover. A cover, like a good title, makes or breaks a book. At any given time there are thousands of books in any bookstore or on any online book portal. What will attract a reader to your book over the others? Unless you're a celebrity or an author of repute, it will be the book cover. Therefore, think about the kind of cover that will do justice to both the content and the sales of your book.

Once your manuscript is ready for publishing, the next (and final) step will be to design the book cover. But why should you be concerned? Isn't this a publisher's prerogative? Yes, your publisher will design a cover for your book, but the truth is that you may not like this cover. Moreover, if you're a female author, you may be given a book cover with stilettos and red lipstick, even if you write serious fiction! Be warned. Many good books have languished because their cover was misleading or uninspiring.

A cover must suit the tone and sensibility of your book, and appeal to your taste. After all, it's your name on it, and you will look at it more than anyone else will (you know you will)! Take out the time, energy, and perhaps money, to get a good cover.

First, you must give a creative brief to your publisher and in-house designer. Be clear about the way you'd like your book cover (front, back, spine and flap) to look. Include what message you want the cover to convey. Don't think of technical aspects like book dimensions, file requirements, specs, tabloid size etc. That's the designer's job. Think theme, colour, tone, message, spine information etc. Research published book covers that may be inspirational for your own book. Send them these images. Send them photos. Send them samples. The creative brief will help your publisher and you match ideas. The publisher's designer will then work on your cover and send you four to five options. If you like either of them, fantastic! You can suggest a few tweaks to the font, colour, picture or text, and everyone is happy. Job finished.

If you don't like the options, then ask for a redo. If those don't work for you, politely ask the publisher if you can, on your budget and time, hire someone else to design your cover. Most publishers don't mind. I know this because two out of my three book covers have been outsourced to and designed by the supremely talented Anurag Hira of One by One Design.

If you reach this stage, first decide which designer you want to use. Apart from Anurag Hira, there are some other popular book cover designers and companies, like: Pinaki De, Aeshna Roy, KS Designers, Seek Red, Ishan Khosla Design, and The Ink Pot. You can Google more. Before hiring a designer, ask for samples of their work. Ask them for their budget (expect to shell out between Rs 5,000-50,000). Send them your creative brief. See if you share visual sensibilities. Connect the designer to the publisher so they can discuss technical aspects.

If you prefer not to spend, you have two options. Make your peace with what the publisher has designed. Or, design your own cover. Learn how to use Canva, Adobe Photoshop, Gimp 2.0, Word, or Adobe InDesign. Use images from vector graphics, public-domain artworks on the web, Flickr, Shutterstock, Pexels, Pixabay, and even Wikimedia. Carefully select the colour scheme, font, picture (if any) and key words. Make sure there are no spelling mistakes! Make sure the book cover pops! Get feedback from friends, social media and websites like PickFu before making the final decision. There is no better time to show the world how multi-talented you are. Make sure that your publisher likes this cover! Good luck!

But before you even begin the cover design process, do these four things:

1. **Confirm Your Book Title:** The publisher may want to change the title of your book and may ask you for four to five other options. Keep these ready. It is equally likely that after editing your book, you may yourself wish to change your title to something that you find more befitting or intriguing. Don't start designing your cover till your title is locked. Remember, the title and cover have to be in sync with each other.

2. **Do Your Research:** Visit a bookstore. Walk through the aisles and pick up books whose covers you're instantly attracted to. Think about what about them you find compelling. These should be your referral points. Pinterest and Amazon are also great places for inspiration.

3. **Get Your Blurbs:** A blurb is advance praise by specialists in your field. The blurb will go on your book cover, and must ideally be added before you begin designing the cover. A good blurb will give your book credibility, especially if it comes from a specialist of repute. Start approaching authors, or experts in your genre, and request them for a blurb. The specialists you approach must be in your genre (imagine a Salman Rushdie giving a blurb for a say Chetan Bhagat book). A blurb from a renowned and credible specialist will hold more meaning than a blurb from a showbiz celebrity, unless you're writing a book on Bollywood. Also, while the publisher may help you procure your blurbs, you will more likely have to rely on your own sources. If you know a specialist personally or have interacted with them on social media or at an event, approach them first. You should ideally request up to ten experts—first, the five who are on your

dream wish list, and later, the five who are lower hanging fruits. This way you'll be able to get two to three blurbs. Begin this process the minute your book contract is signed.

4. **Write Your Book Description:** While most publishers will write a book description for your cover, they may ask you to write it (and then go-ahead and tweak it!). Therefore, keep three versions of your book description ready: a small one (30-50 words), a medium one (50-80 words) and a long one (80-150 words). This can be picked up from the synopsis in your query letter. Though, by this phase of publishing, you may have formed a different idea of your book, so your book description may be slightly different from the one you wrote for the synopsis.

Once these steps are in place, go ahead and design a cover that will make your readers proud to carry your book! You're now a published author! Many congratulations.

How To Self-Publish

DO NOT be disheartened if mainstream publishers reject your book. More than 95% of manuscripts meet the same fate in India and the world over. The reasons for rejection vary from substandard writing to mismatched genres to the publisher's packed publishing schedule to a set of evaluation norms that your book does not abide by. For instance, if your genre is too edgy or disruptive, a traditional publishing house might reject your book fearing that it lacks the potential to scale. If your writing is unique the publisher may become wary of putting you through an arduous and lengthy editing process till the book conforms to their vision.

You can go back to the writing board and rewrite your book, several times if required, as many writers do. If you decide that your book cannot be written any better and that you've done the best that you can, fret not. You can still become a published author. Your book can be sold in bookstores and online, or as an e-book. In today's world the barriers to entry for publishing have been lowered. This is all thanks to self-publishing, a way by which a book can be published without using conventional methods or a traditional publisher.

As a new writer it's alluring to get your book self-published. The do-it-yourself publishing style means that you can bypass the constraints of traditional publishing. You can write exactly what you feel like instead of worrying about what a publisher will be impressed by. You can do what works for you. You do not have to wait for the months or years that it takes for a book to be published via a traditional channel. You can sell your book within minutes, if you so wish. You can upload your book at a nominal cost to a self-publishing platform. You can control every aspect of your book, from the font size to the layout to the design. You can change your text, your book cover and your price, as per the sales of your books, as many times as you want. You get to have complete control over the fate of your book: whether you'd like to print it, whether you'd like to market it. Self-publishing affords you the luxury of not paying for distribution, which means that you can get to keep almost 100% of your royalties after net profits. If your book sells well, you stand to make a lot more money than you would with a traditional publisher. After all, you've invested months or years of your life to write a book. You've harboured dreams of becoming a recognised author. Self-publishing allows you to fulfill those dreams in the easiest possible way.

And there's something in it for everybody. If you write in a local language, you can self-publish your book using Matrubharti or Dailyhunt that specialise in regional content.

No wonder self-publishing is finding more and more takers in India. No wonder a large number of self-publishing platforms have cropped up all over the country.

Here is a list of the major self-publishing platforms in India:
English Language Books – Amazon's Kindle Direct Publishing (KDP), Partridge Publishing (Penguin), The Write Place (Crossword Bookstores), BooksFundr (White Falcon Publishing), Notion Press, Pothi, Cinnamon Teal Publishing, Power Publishers, EBook Sutras, Bookmann India, Kobo, Smashwords, Google Play, Scribd, Become Shakespeare, 24by 7Publishing
Regional Language Books – Dailyhunt, Matrubharti
Academic Books – ScholarGram

Most of these platforms provide the entire spectrum of publishing requirements, from editing to cover designing to printing to distribution to digital marketing services. While most charge a fee, some like KDP are free.

More so, if you're writing short fiction, which find few takers among big publishers, you can use Amazon's Kindle Singles to publish and sell stories. Authors like Amy Tan, Chuck Palahniuk, Susan Hill and Karen Russell have embraced this platform.

The process of self-publishing is fairly straightforward. If everything is in order you can be published in a matter of minutes! After the circuitous publishing route that I've discussed in this book, this sounds so easy and simplistic, right?

Beware! In India, e-books comprise less than a percentage of the Rs 10,000 crore book publishing industry. Since this industry is nascent it's plagued with issues ranging from copyright to sales to distribution and pricing. Some vanity publishers fudge sales data, charge a lot, grab your rights, and create all sorts of problems. Do your research before using a self-publishing platform. Do your due diligence. Check if the platform has an integrated distribution network in the existing book market. Check if they distribute through Amazon and Flipkart. Ask whether they have the ability to distribute in bookstores across India. Check books that the platform has published before. Order these books to check whether the platform lives up to its promise of delivery. Reach out to authors who have self-published to learn about their experience.

Remember, you'll have to spend out of your own pocket in order to publish your book. This can amount to very little or a lot, depending on how you handle the process. On top of that, you'll have to put in a lot of effort and time. While your royalties will be higher as compared to what you'll get with a big publishing house, around 60-70%, the self-publishing platform may take a cut from your royalty. You may not have much to gain monetarily.

Pricing a book right is also a challenge. MRP (Maximum Retail Price)—the index that you see on all products, including books—is calculated based on the type of book i.e. paperback or hardcover, as well as the size of the book i.e. the number of pages. As a rule of thumb books are priced at one rupee per page for paperbacks and 60% of this number for e-books. So, a 300-page book will be priced at Rs 299 as a paperback and Rs 180 as an e-book. You'll have to do a fine balancing act of pricing your book—too low and you'll make no money; too high and you'll find no readers.

You'll also have to, of course, market your own book. If no one knows your book exists, who will buy it? You'll have to identify your target audience and position your book to them. You'll have to be the ambassador of your own book. A self-publishing platform services many authors and does not generally have the bandwidth to promote an individual author. Fret not, this is almost the same scenario for authors who are published traditionally. But your job is tougher because you have to convince a reader to buy your book instead of a book by a reputed publisher or author. You'll have to give the reader something they want.

You will also have to purchase your own ISBN and copyright. ISBN is the 'International Standard Book Number', a unique numeric commercial book identifier required globally to identify a book title. Copyright grants you the exclusive rights for the use and distribution of your original work. While your self-publishing platform may provide you with a unique ISBN number, you are advised not to use this number. In self-publishing whoever owns the ISBN, owns the work. Always buy. It's neither expensive nor difficult.

Keep in mind that you'll also be the gatekeeper of your own writing. You'll have to create a book that's free of spelling mistakes, grammatical gaffes, plagiarism, weak characters and a lack of plot. This will be tough. Even the best writers can rarely spot their own mistakes. Not having objectivity leads to bad books and self-publishing is not a license to write bad books. No one, except your family and close friends, will buy a bad book, even if it is written by you, and in case they do, they'll be turned off and never read anything else that you write. This is not a risk that you should take. Whatever you do you must not ignore this crucial step. Become your toughest critic. If you think you need help, then hire an external editor, or opt for the editing services of the self-publishing platform. It's always better to get a fresh pair of eyes. The good news is that even after your book is published, self-publishing gives you the option to rework and rewrite your book.

While there are a few success stories of self-published authors, from EL James (Fifty Shades of Grey), to Amish Tripathi and Ashwin Sanghi back home, these success stories are rare. You may call yourself a published author but it will do nothing for your writing career if no one reads or respects your work. It may not even make sense for you, if you're writing a literary fiction novel, or a cookbook, or a memoir with photographs, where—due to the complexity of text and formatting—going the traditional way may be better.

Ultimately, even if you are a great writer, if you can't edit, design, proofread or market your book, then self-publishing will do nothing for you. Remember, in self-publishing you are the author and the publisher! Use the skill sets that are required of both and then proceed. As a publisher, you must think like a businessperson. You must reduce costs as much as possible in order to increase profit. But, as an author, you must not compromise on quality. You will lose your reputation before even building one, and then all your efforts will be in vain.

Despite all this, if you still decide to self-publish, then first sit down and set a goal. Are you publishing a book as a vanity project for your family and friends to read, or are you serious about making an impact as an author? Don't waste your time and resources if it's the former. Your family and friends will love and respect you with or without a book; there's no point wasting money and effort just to impress them. If you are serious and have decided to self-publish, select a self-publishing platform that most suits your requirements. See whether you want one that simply lets you sell your book, or one that handholds you through every step of the way i.e. assisted self-publishing.

The rules that apply to standard publishing also apply to self-publishing; so don't be neglectful of those. Take some time to write and edit your book. Write the book that you've always wanted to and write it well. Think of a topic that has a hook and a specific audience so you can sell well. Carefully proofread and edit your manuscript. Before publishing your book, finalize the title, subtitle and book description. Unless you're printing your book, you need a front cover but no back cover design. You can design your cover using the softwares mentioned in the previous chapter: *Design The Perfect Book Cover*. Alternatively, you can hire an expert or utilise the platform's services. Browse through e-books in your genre and study the thumbnails that stand out. Make a thumbnail image for your book that stands out while clearly displaying your book title and genre. Since this will be used across platforms dedicate time to it.

You'll have to choose a size for your book, format your manuscript to fit that size, turn your Word doc into PDF, and upload your book as an e-file to a self-publisher's portal. You can use softwares like Scrivener, Draft2Digital, Press Books, Vellum and Reedsy to convert your word document into an e-file. If you're not tech-savvy then hire a freelancer to do the difficult task of formatting your book and nailing the book specs.

If you want your book in print, in bookstores and on sites like Amazon and Flipkart, then the DIY (do-it-yourself) process gets slightly more rigorous. See if it's worth it. Gauge the reader response to your e-book. If your book is successful as an e-book, it will more likely be successful in print (e-books sell better since they're cheaper). If you manage to make money by selling e-books, you can use that to pay for your print copies. You can then also venture to international agencies like Lulu, Amazon's CreateSpace, Lightning Source, Smashwords and BookBaby, to print your book in foreign markets.

Before printing your book, do an exact page count, and decide the type of layout and paper that can be used for printing. Ensure that your e-book and print edition have the same final text. This is where a good designer or an independent e-book formatting professional can assist you. Alternatively, you can learn how to typeset using publishing software's like Adobe InDesign, SILE, TeX, troff and LaTeX. These will help you design the inside pages of your book for spacing, kerning, tracking controls, density and colour.

Once you're ready to print, you have two options available. One is print-on-demand (POD). POD is a technology that allows you to print one copy of your book at a time. This means that you can print and ship your book only if someone buys it. This way you can gauge how much you'll sell before spending money printing books that no one will buy. The cost of a print-on-demand book is typically quite high, which means that your out-of-pocket expenses will be high and you'll spend more money per copy.

The second option is to use the traditional offset printing press, where you'll print a certain set number of copies. Your cost per book will be lower and you'll have better quality. You can contact a local printer and expect to spend from Rs 100 to Rs 120 per copy. Use this method only if you are certain of selling a certain amount of books, via your network, a store or an institution. Otherwise, keep a few copies of your book in hand, using POD, and scale-up later when you're sure of a demand for your book.

Whatever method you opt for, be careful to make your book look 'professional'. You're going to be competing with books that have taken established publishers months to create. Be aware of what you're up against.

Let's also take a closer look at what self-publishing a book may cost you, if you outsource most of it (please note that these are indicative figures and may vary vastly):

Pre-Production Costs: Editing (20,000) + Cover (10,000) + Typesetting (5,000) + Formatting (5,000) = Rs 40,000

Post-Production Costs: Trailer (25,000)+Book Reviews*5 (75,000)+Newspaper Reviews*2 (20,000)+Social Media Advertising (50,000)+Book Launch *2 (60,000) = Rs 2,30,000

You could end up spending roughly around Rs 2,70,000 to self-publish and market your book. If you price your book at the industry average of Rs 299, 35% of this will offset printing costs (Rs 100-120 per book), while 50% will go as a discount to the bookseller. This will leave you with a gross profit of around 15% per copy, while the net profit will reduce once you include your expenses. On average, you stand to make around Rs 40-50 per book. In order to cover your expenses you will have to sell around 5500-7000 copies. In order to turn a profit you will have to sell more. Your self-publishing platform may not print more than 100-150 copies of your book since, according to industry knowledge, they make money by selling 100 copies of hundreds of thousands of books. This is very different from traditional publishers who try to publish hundreds of thousands of copies of a few books. While these numbers sound low, keep in mind that even established authors in India, published by major publishing houses, have a tough time selling 2000 copies.

You can also distribute your book by yourself but this will involve a lot of hard work and loads of luck! For this you must understand how book distribution in India works. Let's keep it simple. Publishers send their books to distributors. Distributors then send a large number of titles from many different publishers to bookstores. Out of this lot, bookstores pick the books that they think will sell well. It is a complicated system that involves goods and services tax (GST), value-added tax (VAT), point of sale (POS) system integration, and invoices. Due to this, and because they don't anticipate much demand for POD books, bookstores rarely accept them. They also prefer to deal with distributors rather than accept books from individuals. Now you know why it'll be tough getting your book into a brick and mortar store! Additionally, online sellers don't list small presses unless they have 10 or more titles. Or, they may charge an exorbitant fee to list your book, and also take a percentage from each book sold.

If you're self-distributing it might be better to directly approach a distributor instead of a bookstore. Show them the sales reports of your books. Show them good book reviews, both online and offline. Offer them more than what publishing houses do, say 50-60% of the MRP of your book. Bring something to the table that they cannot resist.

If this fails, you have two options.

The first option is to create your own book distribution company. This means that you will print and distribute your own books. Be warned that the returns are, more often than not, sloppy and you must be willing to get the books back if they don't sell. How this helps you is that it gives you direct accessibility to bookstores. As a distributor, you can now talk directly to the representatives. However, this will take convincing, since a bookstore would rather deal with a distributor providing books in bulk rather than one providing a single book. Still, try. Do the hard sales pitch. Try to throw in sweeteners. Think like a businessman.

The second option is simple: you sell your book online by registering yourself as a seller on e-commerce sites. If you sell a lot of books online you may attract the notice of physical stores. This is, as you can imagine, a long shot. Even if you do manage to get this far, your book may not be given the prime shelf space or promotional advantage that say a traditional publisher would get for their catalog.

If you wish to avoid such huge investments of time and money, then self-publishing an e-book will be a better course of action for you. This way you can list your book on Amazon and Kindle, and it can be accessible to a worldwide readership base.

Don't forget that due to the ease of self-publishing everyone and their mother is now a "published" author. The low barriers to entry, the copious number of shoddy books, and the abysmally low success rates have given self-publishing a bad name. It will therefore take a lot for a discerning reader to pick up your book. The silver lining is that if your book is a mega-success, self-publishing can become an opportunity for you to get a publishing contract from a major publishing house.

So, give it everything and keep writing. Be aware. Be smart. The right book finds the right platform.

Publish Short Stories

PUBLISHING WISDOM says that short-story collections don't sell. This is true of India as much as it is around the world. Though more exalted in status than poetry, short stories still find themselves languishing at the bottom of the publishing food chain.

But this century has been good to the short story writer. In 2000, the Grande Dame of short stories, Jhumpa Lahiri, won the Pulitzer Prize for Fiction for her debut collection, *Interpreter of Maladies*. Lydia Davis, whose stories are as short as three pages on average, and some only a sentence long, won the Man Booker International Prize in 2013. Canadian short-story writer Alice Munro, my favourite, won the Nobel Prize in Literature in 2013 for being a 'master of the contemporary short story'. George Saunders won the Folio Prize in 2014 for his collection of short stories, *Tenth of December*. All these wins and trends have taken the literary world by storm and helped delay the death knell for the short story.

Short stories have brought literature down to size. Literally and metaphorically speaking. Today you can tell stories through different mediums. Form does not restrict expression. In 2012, Pulitzer Prize-winning author Jennifer Egan wrote a science fiction short story called *Black Box* in a series of tweets. Indeed: most authors would have been appalled at telling stories in 140 (now 280) character increments and using a medium whose fragmentation precludes storytelling. But she did. And, it was well-received. I'm not surprised. In 2014, I retold the Mahabharata, which is the world's longest epic, in 100 tweets. While the reader and press engagement (national and international) was astounding, what really caught my attention was the unexpected poetry that can happen in 140 (now 280) characters. In Japan, cellphone novels (*keitai shousetsu*), written in the form of text messages, have been bestsellers since the early 2000s. There's accessibility and a certain intimacy in being able to reach people through their phones.

Writing is writing, and what really matters is whether you can tell a good story. So, Eleanor Catton won the Man Booker in 2013 with her 832-page debut, *The Luminaries*. At almost 800 pages, Donna Tartt's, *The Goldfinch*—often described as Dickensian—won the Pulitzer in 2014. The story matters, not its length.

My own experience with short stories has been nothing short of wonderful. Short stories have a strange poetical limitation that makes them fun to read and to write. They unearth a human experience wrapped around a unique experience. When I was writing what would become my debut collection of short stories *Happy Birthday*, every single author and editor told me that I was wasting my time since no one published short stories. The book was picked up by (then) Random House India, longlisted for the world's biggest short story award: *The Frank O'Connor International Short Story Award*, blurbed by authors I revere: Chitra Banerjee Divakaruni called them 'surprising and moving', Jeet Thayil 'deft and merciless', Namita Gokhale as 'possessing intense human sensibility', and Ashwin Sanghi 'provocative and inspirational'. The reviews from both critics and readers were overwhelmingly positive. In 2016, my story *People Of The Sun* won the FON South Asia Short Story Award and I published another collection, *The Trouble With Women* (Juggernaut), which was described as "the best book from Juggernaut" by *The Hindu Business Line*. My short story

Cows That Glow was longlisted for the Commonwealth Short Story Prize (2018). My short stories have been published in over a dozen international literary magazines, including Avatar Review, Wasafari, Eclectica, The Indian Quarterly and QLRS, as well as in anthologies including Namita Gokhale's anthology *The Himalayan Arc*. It's been a long journey from being told I'll never get a single short story published.

So ... listen to your voice. It will guide you to your truth.

Since I've written both novels and short stories, I'm often asked what's the difference between writing the two. This is what I have to say. Imagine getting on a train from Churchgate to Bandra. Imagine meeting a stranger on that train who draws you into a captivating part of her world. Imagine being mesmerised by this stranger. Then her stop comes. The doors open. She steps outside. The doors close. And she's gone. Forever. Imagine that profound feeling that you're left with, of having lost and found something. That's what a short story feels like. It leaves you wanting more. A novel on the other hand, is like a Shatabdi train from Kanyakumari to Kashmir. You cross many milestones, you meet a lot of characters, you exchange life stories, share *mithai* and gossip. When you reach your destination you feel like something inside you has shifted and been fulfilled. Short stories teach us what life is like, where things come and go in a moment's time, while novels fill us up with the fullness of life.

Writing a short story is no different than writing a novel in terms of conception, planning and execution. It is based on your imagination. It has to have a beginning, middle and end. It's opening has to catch the reader's attention and make them want to read more. It has to be driven by a theme or plot or characters. The characters have to speak and behave like we do in real life. The central character has to undergo something—an intriguing and interesting event or experience—which will offer her change. But, within the milieu of a short story, you have a small canvas to work with. So, you have to bring an economy to writing a short story. You have to cut to the bone quickly. Eliminate any unnecessary details, events and circumstances. Keep your dialogues short and absorbing. Don't inhabit your characters in the manner in which you do in a novel. Take the story to its logical conclusion, but—and this is what I love the most about writing short stories—leave a little mystery. The minute the reader finishes reading your short story she must be left yearning for more ... to know what happened next ... to go back and read the story again.

To sum it up, a short story is like an explosion of truth, whereas a novel is like a slow realization of several truths. A short story is about one thing—one facet of human nature, one defining moment, one life-changing experience—while a novel is about many things. In the short story you will sustain a moment, in a novel the plot. Stories are less dutiful than novels because they don't have to stick to a format and everything—the writing, the reading—gets done more quickly. The immersion, the investment of time is not required by the reader with respect to a short story, so they don't build a longitudinal cathexis with the character's world. They enter a mini-world and are ejected from it equally quickly.

Writing a short story is like a fling—short, transformative and captivating; something you reminisce—as compared to writing a novel, which is like a marriage—a committed endeavour that leaves you exhausted and exhilarated at the same time.

If you want to write good short stories, read the masters of the trade, like Alice Munro, O. Henry, Rabindranath Tagore, Jhumpa Lahiri, Tania James, Celeste Ng, Prem Chand, Michael Cunningham, Manto, Raymond Carver, Ismat Chughtai and Junot Diaz. Their stories are a perfect, nuanced, subtle, luminous understanding and expression of people's lives, and of the human heart.

If you're writing a short story collection it will contain anywhere from 10 to 30 stories, each between 2000-8000 words.

Check the websites of publishers listed in Chapter Two: *Identify The Right Publisher* to see which among them is publishing short stories (their requirements vary from year to year). In your submission package to a publisher or agent, you will need: a query letter, a book synopsis (highlight a theme, and four to five of your most hard-hitting stories), three sample stories (check the submission guidelines of the publisher) and your bio.

If you want publishers to take you seriously, try to get your stories published in literary journals and anthologies. Start slowly and build credibility. There are many anthologies you can submit your stories to, by following the social media handles of short story publishers, well-known writers, and literary magazines. Check their call-outs, reading dates, themes, topics and editorial preferences. Submit your story to literary magazines that publish short fiction in India and around the world. Below is a list of magazines that publish Indian writers. Read their submission guidelines online before submitting your story.

International: The New Yorker, The Paris Review, Five Chapters, AGNI, EGO Magazine, Eclectica Magazine, Avatar Review, Wasafari Magazine, Asia Literary Review, The Quarterly Literary Review Singapore (QLRS), Cha: An Asian Literary Journal, A Public Space, Glimmer Train, New England Review, One Story, Ploughshares etc.

National: The Indian Quarterly, The Caravan, The Bombay Review, Muse India, Hans India, Indian Literature (Sahitya Akademi), The Little Magazine, Out of Print Magazine, The Four Quarters Magazine, Pratilipi, Reading Hour, Nether, Open Road Review, Helter Skelter, North-East Review, The Bombay Literary Magazine etc.

Publish Poetry

WHO AMONG us has been unmoved by the plaintive cry of the poet's aphoristic poem? Poems express emotions through thematic metaphor and vivid imagery. They bring us together in our common fate of life's brokenness and heartbreak. Despite this efficacy, poems have failed to find mainstream popularity. The famous poet is as rare as a bestselling poetry collection. It is pitiful, really, that poetry is one of the most neglected art forms in publishing today. But if your dream is to be the next bard of India, then read this chapter.

The first thing you must do as a poet is to develop your style and voice. There are many poetry forms you can choose to write in, from haiku to sonnets to limericks to elegies to free verse to couplets to villanelles. Before you approach a mainstream publisher, you must build your credentials and reputation. Beef up your social media reach. Publish your poems online. Enter as many poetry competitions as you can. Get some fans. Be deeply entrenched in the poetry community, both offline and online. You can do this by attending and participating in poetry festivals, poetry readings, poetry slams, open mics, poetry sessions and poetry clubs.

Read the work of admirable poets who've weaved words through aeons, whether it's contemporary poets like Arundhathi Subramaniam, Jeet Thayil, Tishani Doshi, Ranjit Hoskote, Meena Kandasamy, Vikram Seth, Gulzar, or classical poets like Rabindranath Tagore, Harivansh Rai Bachchan, Mahadevi Verma, Sumitranandan Pant, Sarojini Naidu, Dom Moraes, K. Sachidanandan, Adil Jussawalla, or W.B.Yeats, Dante, Shakespeare and T.S. Eliot.

Send your poems to literary magazines. In India these include *The Little Magazine, The Caravan, Antiserious, Vayavya, Helter Skleter Magazine, Cha: An Asian Literary Journal, Open Road Review, Indian Literature, North-East Review, Muse India, The Bombay Review,* and *Indian Review.*

Poetry books suffer from low visibility (there's hardly a bookstore with a separate poetry section), patchy distribution (hardly any bookstores want them), and poor sales. Since the risk-appetite in publishing has gone down, publishers prefer books that have a higher probability of flying off the shelves. Only a handful of publishers still publish poetry collections. So, if you are a new poet, be prepared to hear a lot of: "We don't publish poetry" or "We will print if you pay" or "Poetry doesn't sell". Bigger publishers rarely accept poetry manuscripts, except for say Penguin, or Aleph (no unsolicited manuscripts), so you can approach newer publishers, like Rumour Books India or Kitaab, publish through The (Great) Indian Poetry Collective, or self-publish (See *Chapter Two: How To Self-Publish*). Do your research and due diligence.

For poetry submissions, publishers typically require a brief synopsis, author bio, and five sample poems. Again, make sure to check submission guidelines before sending a query letter. There is no definitive rule for length, but a poetry book on average contains around 50-80 poems with a total word count of 15,000, and each poem must be a page or two long.

There are many anthologies and compendiums in which you can publish your poems. Follow the social media handles of poetry publishers, well-known poets, poetry editors and literary magazines, so you don't miss their call-outs, reading dates, themes, topics and editorial preferences.

And, here's some good news. Due to the nearly closed doors of traditional publishers, poets are increasingly uploading their poems online. This has given rise to a new breed of poets, called Instapoets, who are publishing verses primarily on social media. These are typically minimalistic and bite-sized free verses written simply, with erratic line breaks, and without punctuation. The focus is not as much on content and form as on honesty, authenticity, transparency, and relatability. The reader has to enter or feel like she's entering the personal life of the poet, as she would with a friend. The poet's success therefore depends on likeability and virality. The trailblazer for this trend has been Rupi Kaur whose poetry collections have sold in millions around the world.

These young poets are drawing criticism for producing what many say are vapid and disingenuous texts, which sound like bumper stickers, or doodles in margins of schoolbooks, or musings in the guise of poetry. These poets are being accused of hailing the death of poetry by confusing accessibility with talent. The poets defend themselves, saying that they're reimagining poetry and nursing it back to life. The truth is that digital media gives poets a platform for outreach and instant gratification that traditional publishing does not.

Ultimately, art lies in the eyes of the beholder. Art is always far greater than its platform. If you have a voice, use that voice, no matter what the medium or reaction.

Publish Non-Fiction

AS THE word suggests non-fiction is a narrative form dealing with fact-based and real-life events, people and information, versus fiction, which is partly or largely imaginary. If you're planning to write non-fiction, you've tapped the deep end of the pool, my friend. This is because non-fiction in India (and the world over) sells better than fiction, better than short stories, better than poetry, even better than commercial fiction (well, almost). This is because people read fiction for pleasure (not a priority) and non-fiction for survival (definitely a priority).

Non-fiction books are generally divided into the following broad categories. The first popular category contains autobiographies (your life story written by you), biographies (your life story written by someone else) and memoirs (part of your life story written by you, drawn from memory rather than fact). These are books about people in the limelight who have accomplished something against all odds. The presence of a *neta*, *abhineta* or cricketer almost guarantees a bestseller. Think of *The Story Of My Experiments With Truth* (Mahatma Gandhi), *Autobiography of An Unknown Indian* (Nirad Chaudhuri), and *Rekha: The Untold Story* (Yasser Usman). Then there's the incredibly popular self-help or self-improvement category. People always need (or think they need) help to sort out their life, their work, their heartbreaks, their diets, their public speaking ... the list is endless. They like access to expert wisdom

123

without spending too much (who wouldn't?), which is why such books are a huge draw. If you want to change people's lives, this is the category you should write in. Example of such books are *The Monk Who Sold His Ferrari* (Robin Sharma), *You Can Win* (Shiv Khera) *You Are Born To Blossom* (A.P.J. Abdul Kalam), and *Don't Lose Your Mind, Lose Your Weight* (Rujuta Diwekar). Then there are guides, manuals, handbooks and technical books that cover information about a particular subject matter in depth, say computer software. Historical writing (a study of the past) is a big draw in our country with renowned books like *India After Gandhi* (Ramachandra Guha) and *India Unbound* (Gurcharan Das). Travel is somewhat popular and divided into travelogues (your journey to a particular place), travel literature (guide books) and travel fiction (travel stories using elements of creative fiction). Think of *City of Djinns* (William Dalrymple) and *The Heat And Dust Project* (Devapriya Roy). Then there's creative non-fiction or literary non-fiction where literary devices are used to create non-fiction narratives, like the must-read *Our Moon Has Blood Clots* (Rahul Pandita) and *Dongri to Dubai: Six Decades Of The Mumbai Mafia* (S. Hussain Zaidi).

Before you begin writing non-fiction ask yourself if you're the right person for this job. Are you an expert on this subject matter? Do you know enough to pass on this knowledge to others? Also, decide what your book is about (remember, elevator pitch), who you're targeting, whether your book will add value, and whether you have enough content to fill the book.

Writing non-fiction does not preclude creativity or personality or good writing. Yes, you're presenting data, facts, concepts and analysis, but you're also *writing*. Think like a writer. Make your book engaging. To begin with, you have it easier than fiction writers. You're not creating a whole new world; you're presenting the real world. Don't be lazy. Like with fiction, begin each chapter with a hook. Use a personal story, a historical story, an interesting or funny thought, or ask a relevant question. Do not be overtly factual or prosaic. Write simply so that a 10-year-old or a 100-year-old can read your book (see *Chapter One: Don't Overwrite*). If you want to develop your skills as a non-fiction writer then write non-fiction articles for newspapers, magazines or websites, or write research papers for academic journals.

There are some writers—like Truman Capote, Manu Joseph, Chimamanda Ngozi Adichie or Teju Cole—who can tread both waters, of fiction and non-fiction writing, skillfully. Most writers can't. Read their work for inspiration.

In your submission package to a publisher or agent, you will need: your sub-genre (pick from the categories above), a table of contents (see the index of this book as an example), chapter synopsis, two to three sample chapters (see the submission guidelines of the publisher), and a marketing plan on how you'll sell the book. As I've stated before, if you are a new author, keep your polished manuscript ready *before* you send your query letter, so you can shoot it off in case a publisher expresses interest. To see what to include in your query letter and submission package, read the chapters *How To Write A Query Letter* and *Get Your Submission Package Ready*.

Fortunately for you, almost all major publishers accept non-fiction proposals (see *Chapter Two: Identify The Right Publisher*) so send out your non-fiction proposal to all and watch the red carpet roll out!

CHAPTER THREE

MARKETING

People don't buy what you do; they buy why you do it. And what you do simply proves what you believe.
— *Simon Sinek, Start With Why: How Great Leaders Inspire Everyone To Take Action*

Why You Need To Market Your Book

IT'S EASIER to get published now that it's ever been in India's history, but it's also never been this difficult to sell books. Whether you plan to write the next Man Booker winner or a summer beach read, one thing has changed for certain: the days of the author's ivory tower are over. You have to sell as much as you have to write. You have to treat yourself as a brand and your book as a product. You have to be accessible to your reader. You have to be a shameless self-promoter. This is a fundamental truth that many people are not aware of. The biggest challenge in publishing today is discoverability. Your book will not sell unless you sell it. That's where marketing comes in.

One day in the jungle a lion roared. All the animals ran helter skelter in fear. A rabbit observed this and thought to himself that if the lion could rule the jungle with one roar ... well, so could he! What was the big deal? The next day, the rabbit raised his head and, in imitation of the lion, he let out a roar. Of course, all he managed to get out was a feeble squeak. The other animals laughed at him. The lion walked up to the rabbit and killed him with one stroke of his powerful paw. This powerful advertising anecdote teaches us that we must advertise our goods only if we actually *have* the goods to deliver.

Due to the decolonisation of literature, the large number of publishers, and options other than traditional publishing, the barriers to entry into publishing have lowered. It's easier to get published now that it's ever been in India's history. Homegrown and foreign publishing houses are now publishing Indian authors in droves. The problem with this scenario is that while it's become easy to get published, it's become difficult to sell books. There are too many books, too many authors, and—comparatively—too few readers. The biggest obstacle a new writer will face after finding a suitable publisher is finding a loyal base of readers.

Why? Because there are 82,000 new books that get published in India every year, of which around 22,000 are in English, and only 2% of these books make it to bookstores. And you're not just competing with these books. There are around 2.2 million books that get published globally every year. 75 million books already exist on this planet. So, while a bookstore may stock around 2000 books on average, they will also have a backlist. On top of that, brick and mortar bookstores stock 20% books and 80% merchandise—chocolates, watches, pen nibs, greeting cards, coffee beans and toys etc. This means that a bookstore has even less shelf space for books. So what kind of books will they keep in this limited shelf space? Obviously … the ones that sell. Even on online bookstores, say a Flipkart, your book will not be seen, unless a reader goes to the search engine and types your book's name. 40% of sales happen this way.

The bigger problem is that, in today's world, you're not just competing with other books or other authors. You are also competing for people's time. You are competing to get that reader off his phone, off Twitter, off Whatsapp, to pick up your book and take out the time to read your book. You are competing with movies, plays, comedy shows, iPad's, video games, Netflix, Amazon Prime, Peppa Pig, Taylor Swift, the 10,000 movies that come out every year, and the 75,000 music albums that come out every year.

There's a criticism of the Indian writing scene that, in recent years, there's been almost no great writing at all. Yes, since more than a decade, the success of mass-market books have brought rapid changes in an industry that was earlier driven by the literary lineage of Salman Rushdie, Amitav Ghosh and Arundhati Roy. But don't forget that India is a land of historic storytelling. Our country will always produce great storytellers. Look at the body of work by Aravind Adiga, Rohinton Mistry, Arundhati Roy, Salman Rushdie, Padma Viswanathan, Manu Joseph, Akhil Sharma, Chitra Banerjee Divakaruni, Deepti Kapoor, among others. We have enough diversity, anarchy and mysticism to provide inspiration to scores of good writers. There are enough good writers and enough good books. The problem is not a lack of good books, but a lack of good books not finding mainstream popularity. This is what is creating the perception of a paucity of good writing.

Let's take a look at one of the biggest selling literary phenomenon in the world today: J.K. Rowling. After the unprecedented success of *Harry Potter* the author wrote *Cuckoo's Calling* under the pseudonym Robert Galbraith. The same penmanship, the same genius was brought back on paper. But the book sold only 1500 copies worldwide. Compare this to the 500 million and counting copies she'd sold of *Harry Potter*. Rowling was left with little choice, I imagine, than to step up and take ownership of writing *Cuckoo's Calling*. No points for guessing how sales of the book spiked. This shows us that the biggest challenge in publishing today is discoverability, not just in India but worldwide. A good book does not sell by itself. The challenge is to connect the right author with the right audience. That's where marketing comes in.

I wish I could tell you that your book would speak for itself. That your writing would shine through all the clutter and noise. Before I entered this industry, I believed that writing is sacred and marketing a book is sacrilegious. That was until I realised that my book will not sell unless I sell it. The truth is that in today's world books are treated as products because they are acquired, priced, distributed, sold, and priced. Sadly, in today's world, selling a book is no different than selling soap or toothpaste. Literature is no longer about the book as much as the author. The author is no longer a delicate genius who is read but not seen. Blowing your own trumpet is no longer associated with a lack of substance. Today, to be considered a successful author, you have to have more marketing prowess than writing prowess. This is underscored by the fact that businessmen, as well as people with MBAs, and marketing degrees, are selling the most books ... they know how to 'position' their books. In India today, if you write well, and market well, you can use publishing as a life-changing opportunity.

So, what can you do? How can you create brand recall for your book? How can you ensure that your book doesn't vanish into oblivion? Let's find out.

What's A Bestseller?

THE TERM 'bestseller' for Indian fiction is a relatively new concept. It came about in 2004 when a banker named Chetan Bhagat published a tale about campus romance in *Five Point Someone*. Despite drawing literary flak, he achieved what India had never seen before: the bestselling phenomenon for local Indian authors writing in Indian English.

His success has spawned this Habeas Corpus state of affairs in publishing where many authors are claiming to write bestsellers without proof or veracity. Since there's no accountability or transparency in the publishing system, no one actually knows which book is a bestseller. Such news is either spread through the grapevine, or, more often than not, by the concerned author. No wonder, calling yourself a bestselling author in India today has acquired a farcical tone. So, if you become a bestselling author, it'll be best to back your boasts with numbers or photos.

Let's take a look at some numbers: 90% of all books published in India sell less than 2000 copies every year. A paltry 9% sell between 2000 to 10,000 copies, and—hold your breath—less than 1% sell more than 10,000 copies. While this number sounds ridiculous, considering we are a population of almost a billion and a half, a book is typically considered a bestseller when it crosses this coveted 10,000 mark within a year of its publication. Despite our technological advances, digital revenue is still only 3.4% of total sales. While India may have 22 official languages and 1600 regional ones, 55% of all books sold are written in English and 35% in Hindi. The regional language penetration of books across India is meager, sadly so.

Most bestsellers today have a cut and paste formula—write in simple language, put a finger on the pulse of modern urban Indian life, devise fast-paced narratives with plenty of emotions and drama, identify a specific market, target the customer, keep the price point of the book between rupees ninety-nine to one hundred and fifty, market well, and, most importantly, track the product.

It's rather worrisome that literature in India has become this formulaic. Authors are cashing in on trends like IIM-IIT campus novels or mythology or self-help books, and no one is pushing the envelope. If nothing new is being said or written, books in India will not have any transformative or evocative power. This will lead to Indian writing becoming too secure, too staid. It will take focus away from writing good books to selling bad books. In this way, the bestselling phenomenon corrupts writing. It focuses on gaming the system, instead of adding something of value to the system. It makes the bestselling authors focus on numbers instead of stories. This trend merits examination and begs for change.

Our country deserves better literature.

As you begin your writing journey, make sure that this greed for money and fame, for making the "bestseller list", doesn't stop you from creating good stories.

Your Marketing Plan

WHAT'S THE secret to marketing your book successfully? Well, the first thing I'd advice—and I'm not alone here—is to come up with a marketing plan well before your book is published. In fact, come up with Plan A and B and C and D etc. When you're trying to convince readers to buy your book, you have to prepare yourself for failures, roadblocks and setbacks. You need contingency plans. You have to be at your creative best.

These are usual steps that new and ambitious authors take to promote their book:

a. Incessantly pushing their book on social media
b. Desperately convincing everyone they meet, even strangers, to buy their book
c. Hosting a flurry of book launches and readings
d. Hiring a PR agency, if they're rich or naïve

According to publishing folklore, these strategies do not help anyone sell more than a few hundred copies. Why? If you spend a few lakhs to get your book covered on Page 3 of a newspaper, what are the odds of a serious reader (and not social-climber) seeing it? What is the point of spending on a book launch, if only your family and friends—who'd anyway buy your book or ask for a free copy (sigh!)—show up to your book launch? What's the point of persistently pushing your book on Facebook when most of your 'friends' will end up muting, unfollowing

135

or unfriending you? What's the point of doing a book reading where only four people will show up?

Since there are too many variables and not enough data, you can spend a lot of money on book marketing without knowing whether it's had any impact on your book sales. Still, if you're going to spend money, spend it wisely. Here are some avenues you can explore to generate organic readers, create a buzz about your book without annoying people (and even if you do, it's ok), and sell more book copies.

Having a social media profile helps you only to a certain extent. To truly make an impact, you'll have to adopt new media. Identify where your target audience is most likely to be and be present there. For example, if you're writing campus or romance or young adult novels, it will help to be where the young ones are. So, join sites like Tumblr and Snapchat where you can be accessible to your target audience and 'hang out' with them.

There are paid platforms where you can market your book, like Facebook ads, Amazon advertising, Google AdWords, YouTube advertising, Instagram Influencer Marketing, Goodreads ads, Twitter ads, email blasts and social media post boosts. The conversion rate on Instagram, Goodreads, YouTube and Twitter is said to be minimum. Email blasts and boosted posts on social media are good, but not good enough to make a dent. So, use Facebook Ads, Amazon Advertising and Google AdWords more, as you can really make an impression. Track your ads using performance tools like Kissmetrics or Google Analytics, so you know you're not wasting your money.

Place books ads not only on book blogs, but also on subject-related blogs. If you're writing about crime, find a similar blog where people interested in that subject matter and hence in your book will most likely be present.

Get an email list of Amazon's top reviewers who have indicated their interest in reviewing books from here: www. amazon.com/review/top-reviewers. Get their email ID's manually from their profile page or through websites like

AMZDiscover or Salesbacker. Start emailing these reviewers three to four months before the launch. Customise your email to each reviewer using his or her first name. Ask them to review your book on Amazon, Goodreads, Flipkart, Twitter, Facebook, and any book blogs/clubs you can think of. If they confirm their interest, send them a copy of your book. Don't spend thousands of your precious author rupees on physically mailing your book to these people. Don't send them a PDF file either because this can be uploaded on the Internet. Instead, upload your book on NetGalley: www.netgalley.co.uk/request_terms. You can send a polite reminder about the expected review a month later, and another one two-three weeks later. There's not much else you can do beyond this, so focus on the reviews that you do get. A few weeks before the launch, you should hopefully have some reviews on Goodreads (don't forget to create a book page), and many more by the launch month.

If you want to market your book on Facebook, then spend a little money and use a Facebook ad. Specify your target audience. Select people who are reading books in genres similar to yours, or whose interests correspond with your book. Target an audience size between 0.5-1.5 million. But people rarely click on sales links. Why should they? You'll have to find a way to get them to. Make sure your ad contains the following. First: a testimonial. Select a newspaper review, an author blurb, or an Amazon review. Back this up with either statistics to prove that your book is selling, or has achieved something (an award, five-star reviews on Amazon, thousand likes on the book's Facebook page, etc.) Put a link where people can buy your book. Make an offer they can't resist, like a 'sale ends today' or 'limited stocks only'. Be creative. If you can afford it, get a professional to help you with online optimisations and tweaks.

An email click rate is much higher than a Facebook, Twitter or Instagram click rate. Email lists typically show a conversion rate between 1-5%, so if you have a database of 10,000 folks, you can sell 500 copies. Compare this to Facebook that has a conversion rate of less than 1%. So, instead of spending hours on social media in the hope that your Twitter followers and Facebook 'friends' will buy your book, you can spend time on something that'll convert to actual sales: people you've met or people who share similar interests as you. Remember the business cards you dump in the trash the minute you get home from a networking event? Stop. Instead, note down the contact's number on your phone and put their email in a mailing list. Start building your database of influencers, journalists and reviewers around six months before your book is published. Make a list with names, organisations, emails and numbers on an excel sheet so you remain organised. Over time you'll build a large subscriber base. These are people who will, most likely, share similar interests as you and could be your potential readers. Don't just send them your book links. Build a relationship with them as you would with a friend. Once every month, or quarter, send them something they can use, like a newsletter with tips for writing, tricks to get followers, your articles and short stories, your opinion on different issues. Share something about yourself. Treat them as your friend and not subscriber. Let them know the person behind the author. If they like and/or respect you, they'll be more likely to click on the link to buy your book. This is much more effective than cold reach-outs. Don't forget to use a service like MailChimp or Zoho to store your email database, otherwise you'll spend days just sending out emails.

If you're spending on marketing your book, then don't expect this to be sponsored by your advances or royalties, or by your publisher. Most of your marketing expenses will come from your own pocket. It's a risk. You can mitigate this risk to a certain extent by writing a good book. Because even if you spend lakhs on flashy newspaper ads, or book tours with cheese and champagne, no one will buy or read your book unless it's written well. Secondly, unless you're a rich businessman or celebrity who can keep pumping in money for book marketing, you'll have to rely on word-of-mouth to sell your book. This will happen only if you've written a good book. Lastly, expect to lose money to sell your first 10,000 copies, but if you cross that mark and your book is good, then word-of-mouth and positive online reviews will be ample to ramp up your sales, increase your royalties and—if you're lucky—get you a movie deal. Focus on that initial thrust.

The Best Marketing Tools

BELOW I'VE listed some of the best tools and practices in book marketing today. Some of them are free; most of them are not. The short-term loss to your pocket will hopefully be compensated by a long-term increase in sales. Any marketing is a risk, of course, for a lot depends on the quality of your book, the reach that you are able to gain, and—at the end, like everything else in life—plain dumb luck. So, good luck!

Website: It's useful to have an author website for many reasons. It's probably the first thing that will pop up when your name is Googled. This way you can control the first impression you make on a reader, publisher or journalist. It's the perfect platform for you to showcase your books and yourself in the best positive light. You can post links for interested readers to buy your book. You can put bonus content, merchandise, a newsletter, a behind-the-scenes look to the creative process, or a Twitter feed. You can put a way for people to interact with you and get in touch with you. Be creative. Showcase the site with your voice and personality. Most importantly, make that BUY NOW button pop. Get a professional if you need to. Don't go overboard and spend a lot of money, though. There are many services online that offer domain name registration, a hosting account and a template for little or no money. You can use WordPress, Joomla!, Drupal, GoDaddy, Wix, Seek Red, or Webnode. For inspiration, study the websites of Amy Krouse

Rosenthal, Roxane Gay, J.K. Rowling, E.L. James, Gillian Flynn, Jerry Pinto, Vikram Chandra, Tabish Khair, Vikas Sawrup, Chitra Banerjee Divakurni, Amitav Ghosh and Shashi Tharoor.

Book Excerpts: An effective way to pique the interest of the readers is to give away free excerpts of your book to bookstores or on different book platforms, like book clubs and blogs. Continue to do so, if you can, before and after your book is launched.

Book Community: Involve yourself in the writing community. Meet and reach out to other writers by reading their book and sharing (positive) feedback. Join book clubs in your city or town (like Caferati, Bombay Book Club, Goodreads, Mumbai Book Club, The PEN, The Gurgaon Connection Book Club, The Delhi Book Club etc). Be involved with book launches, book fests and literature festivals where you can directly interact with other authors and readers.

Free Copies: You can set aside 500-1000 copies of your book to give away to influencers and reviewers in your genre. You can give them away at book signings, book readings, literature festivals, on Goodreads, or during social media campaigns. This way you can hope to garner interest and a positive word-of-mouth that will create some sort of impact for your book. Giving away copies to libraries is also a good idea. This will not affect the sales of your book, but it will lend you credibility, and create a new reader database.

Blogging: Blogging no longer enjoys the exalted status it did a few years ago, but if you enjoy maintaining a blog and having loyal readers, then let no trend stop you. A blog can help you hone your writing skills, develop a specialised topic, create a fan base, and engage with your audience. Do give as good as you get, and engage with other bloggers by leaving feedback and sharing your links.

Book Trailers: Do you even need a book trailer? The verdict is not yet out on that. A good book trailer is easy to consume, easy to share, can buff up your YouTube presence, lend your book a multimedia dimension, and can make your book stand out. A bad book trailer can hurt you. It can put off potential readers, take away from the reader's imagination, and not give any real ROI (return on investment). A book trailer can help you intrigue a potential reader and arouse their visual, auditory and emotional senses, only if the video is outstanding … and that is expensive. Unless you have deep pockets to pay someone to make a professional film for you, or you have a friend who is a director, you can either skip this step or learn how to do this by yourself. You can make a basic book trailer using free softwares like Windows Movie Maker, Animoto, Movavi, Blender and iMovie. You will need a script, a background score, images, graphics etc. Try to avoid putting yourself or an amateur actor in the trailer. It will look caricaturish. Before you go down this road, think carefully about whether a book trailer is worth your time, effort or money. The probability of a book trailer going viral is virtually nil.

Amazon: One of the best tools to market your book, something that most authors ignore is the Amazon page. Pay attention. This is where the reader will come to decide whether or not she wants to buy your book. It's also the first impression the reader will have of you as a writer. Make it count. Your first step will be to create an *Author Central* account on your Amazon page (https://authorcentral.amazon.com). You can create an author profile that is both unique and genuine. Put up a video about your book or of you as an author. Upload a blog link. Share a book interview you've done. Help your book come into the limelight using features like tags, listmania, reader reviews and any other features that may be useful. Intrigue the reader. Boost your Amazon profile. This feature is doubly beneficial because this is where you can take stock of your book sales, study sales trends, get tips and build reviews. Amazon also has a *Meet the Authors* forum where you can introduce yourself and ask for reviews. It has an audio book section called *Audible*. Try to get your book placed there so readers can listen to your book.

Amazon Giveaway is also a great way to use the website as an author. Here's another tip. For a limited time, *Kindle* will make your book freely available. Use this to the best extent that you can. Compel people to download your book for free! This will help you capture a new readership base, and every free download will count as a sale!

Movie Deals: If a movie producer or film production company approaches you saying they want to convert your book into a film, congratulations! This is the chance for your book to reach lakhs of people. This is a way for you to immortalise your characters. A word of caution: don't rush into the first offer made to you. Yes, it is exciting. Yes, your book sales might skyrocket. Yes, you want your book to become a *Three Idiots*. But that doesn't mean you behave like one. The film industry is much more opaque and ruthless than the publishing industry. There are far too many gatekeepers between the story and the audience, plagiarism is a massive issue, writers are at the bottom of the pecking order, and there are huge teams involved every step of the way who will change your story beyond recognition. Protect yourself and your story; hire an entertainment lawyer or get a helpful friend in the industry to help you navigate tricky and layered film contracts. Don't get taken for a ride. Make sure you get your due in terms of money and credit.

Write Articles: If you want to build your profile as an author then consider writing articles and opinion pieces on topics that interest you. For example, as a feminist, I am vociferous in my opinion related to gender equality. As a result, I have written over one hundred articles for all the major newspapers, magazines, websites and news portals across the country. I have also written about books, writing, travelling, dating, food, motherhood, love, politics, humour and just about anything else under the sun. The best part is that you don't have to be a journalist to be able to write articles (think Twinkle Khanna or Anand Neelakantan). The biggest challenge you will face in this journey is to establish yourself as a credible columnist. Your first step must be to hone in on what your area of specialisation is. Simply put, what do you want to write about? Once you've determined that, make a list of publications that will be interested in your particular topic. Go to their websites and read their submission guidelines. Pitch to them accordingly. Don't send an article about geriatric ailments to a youth website. Don't send an article on male humour to a feminist website. Know your audience. If there is no information online then ask a friend in that publication to connect you to the right editor. If you have no leads, then be shameless and send a Facebook message or tweet to the editor-in-charge. At the worst, they'll ignore your message. Once you have a contact, email your article pitch to the editor. This pitch will contain the article title, three to four sentences summarising the article, and your one-line bio. Make sure that the editor's name is correctly spelt. If the editor likes your idea they will ask you to send the full article, while giving you a sense of the word count, deadline and fees. Some publications pay, others don't, especially to a new columnist. See what works for you. Once you build a file of stories and make a name for yourself, you can get paid anywhere between Rs 4 to Rs 25 per word. Some publications pay a flat fee usually in the amount ranging from Rs 3,000 to Rs 8,000. Make sure that once your article is published you promote it on social media. Some of India's most popular publications that accept freelancers are Times of India, Hindustan Times, DNA, MidDay, Outlook, The Asian Age, Mumbai Mirror, Tehelka, Vogue, Harper's Bazaar, Verve, Cosmopolitan, Grazia, Man's World, India Today, Scroll, Firstpost, The Huffington Post, DailyO and BuzzFeed. Google for more. While joining the rank of India's top columnists is no easy task, it is doable with hard work, persistence and, like all things, a whole lot of talent.

Awards: Make sure that your publisher sends your book to the relevant book awards. Winning awards, or even being shortlisted or longlisted for them, will give you credibility and coverage.

These are some of the awards for novels: Jnanpith Award, Sahitya Akademi Award, Yuva Puraskar, Crossword Book Award, Saraswati Samman, Tata Literature Live! Awards, The DSC Prize for South Asian Literature, the Shakti Bhatt First Book Prize, Vyas Samman, Bharat Nirman Award, Muse India Young Writer Awards, Rabindranath Tagore Literary Prize, and The Hindu Literary Prize. Many of these awards cover poetry and non-fiction as well.

For your book on poems, you can submit to: the All India Poetry Competition, the National Poetry Competition, and the International Poetry Competition. If you write short stories you can submit them for scores of prizes like the Commonwealth Short Story Prize, Write India Contest (Times of India), the James White Award, Aeon Award, Writer's Digest Annual Writing Competition, The New Asian Writing Short Story Competition, American Short(er) Fiction Prize, ABR Elizabeth Jolley Short Story Prize, Mslexia Women's Fiction Awards, the Harper's Bazaar Short Story Competition, and Bristol Short Story Prize.

How To Use Social Media

BE PRESENT on social media but don't waste precious hours whiling away your time on it, time that you could spend writing. For example, I dedicate fifteen minutes in the morning, fifteen minutes in the afternoon, and fifteen minutes late evening to social media. On days that I'm writing it's less, a few minutes a day, if at all. Other authors dedicate much more or much less time, while some have chosen not to be present on social media at all.

You must first decide whether or not you want a social media presence. After that, you must allocate the time spent on social media with your ROI on it. Is tweeting helping you build credibility as an opinion maker? Is Facebook helping you connect with people from the publishing world? Is Instagram helping you share your life as an author? Find a reason to be on social media (not for time-pass). Your purpose must be to learn, engage and contribute. Be productive. At the same time, don't use it only to post links of your books or articles. Would you follow someone who *only* talks about themselves? Mix it up. Share excerpts of your book. Ask for opinions on your book title. Get your followers to give you suggestions on your book cover. Your followers want to know the person behind the author. Be generous. Give as good as you get. Share links about possible residencies, awards and fellowships. Share tips. Share links to writing competitions. Don't hesitate to ask questions about publishing or writing. With the pace with which the world changes it's impossible to stay abreast of everything, so there are no stupid questions, even if you are an established author. You'll be surprised at how willing people are to help out and give insights if you've made an effort to interact with them in a positive way. Join writers groups. Upload your videos on YouTube. They don't have to be professionally shot as long at they provide some information or insight to the viewer. Raise your profile.

Even if you're not getting many likes or retweets at first, be tenacious. Once you've developed an online voice and profile, the likes and retweets will come. Remember, everything you do creates a digital footprint, so think before you post. It will shape your reputation as a certain kind of writer. You might think no one is watching ... everyone is. Even if they don't engage, everyone has their eyes on everyone else. That's the whole point of social media. Proceed with this in mind.

There are many authors who get tempted to buy Twitter or Facebook or Instagram followers or likes or views. While this may boost your ego, it may do nothing for you in terms of book sales or gaining new readers. In fact, it may be counter-productive because in most cases plumped-up profiles are fairly obvious. A debut author with no prior claim to fame, but 100,000 Twitter followers and low engagement rates, will be called out as a fake. The choice is yours but buying your way through social media may ultimately be a waste of your money.

You must follow authors and personalities who you find inspiring. Your timeline must be filled with people who make you want to get up and reach for the stars! If you want to know how to write your book, then study the works of literary fiction authors. If you want to know to sell your book, then study the social media strategy of popular commercial fiction authors. Commercial fiction authors like Ravinder Singh, Durjoy Datta, Shobhaa De and Chetan Bhagat are prominent on Twitter. You can also follow international authors like J.K Rowling,

Neil Gaiman, Teju Cole and Margaret E. Atwood, whose accounts provide the heady mixture of entertainment and insight, just like their books.

Make your presence felt! Let your personality shine! Let your opinion count!

But ultimately you are a writer, not a performer or a celebrity, so while social media may help you, nothing will count for as much as your writing. Be smart.

How To Get Book Reviews

GETTING YOUR book reviewed will be one of the most tedious parts of book marketing. You'll have to plan and work hard. Ultimately, a good review or few will make it worth it. Try to get as many reviews as you can *before* and *after* your book is launched. This way, by the time your book is published, you can use any flattering quotes to give your book a push and create a buzz.

There are some popular book blogs and bloggers that your publisher or you can approach, like the Hungry Reader, IndiBlogger, Indianbloggers, BlogAdda, Writersmelon, The Readers Cosmos, Arvind Passey, Sarath Babu, Vandana Choudhary, Nimi Vashi, Aathira Jim, Vivek Tejuja and Tarang Sinha.

These are just a few names. Google and reach out to more book bloggers and journalists in your genre. Go to Goodreads, Facebook or Blogspot book groups, and other social media platforms. There is a problem of plenty among bloggers and only a few of them have a big loyal following. To be safe you can check their MozRank (the popularity score of any website) and vet them out. Shortlist names. See if there's a synergy. If you're writing mythology, make a list of people who review books of mythological writers like Amish Tripathi, Devdutt Patnaik and Ashwin Sanghi. Write them a customised email. Let them know that you are aware of their work due to which they might be interested in reading yours. Pitch your book to them, mention the format and date of publication, and offer a free copy for review. Many times you may not receive a reply. You can send a short follow-up email and leave it at that. If someone replies, be meticulous about sending your book to them. Do not ask for a positive review. Trust in your talent to take its own journey. Be patient. Reviewers take time. If you receive a negative review, don't confront the reviewer. Every person will experience your book differently. It's impossible for everyone to like your book. Also, some bloggers will ask money to review your work, upwards of Rs 1000. Unless you're going through a PR company or have a big marketing budget, do not use them. Caveat Emptor.

If you want to see your book reviewed the old-fashioned way—in print—then you'll have to approach newspapers, magazines and literary journals. Be aware that the print space for reviews has shrunk so much over the years that it's virtually non-existent. Persist. Find the ones who are still doing reviews at the time your book is released. Learn how the process works. Your publisher will send your book to their database of media contacts. Make sure you ask them for this list. If you think that any newspaper or magazine or website has been left out, point it out. Publishers are typically happy to expand their list. If they're unwilling to send your book to more reviewers, then buy a few author-discounted copies (you'll get very few free copies of your own book!) and send these out yourself with a nicely written introduction letter. If you have friends who are journalists, request them to introduce you to the book review department in their organisation. There seems to be a misnomer that you can get newspaper reviews only if you pay money. I know authors who do that, of course, but these authors have low self-esteem, deep pockets, or terribly written books. If your book is well-written and you possess a strong voice, you will get reviewed—for free! I know this because major newspapers and magazines have reviewed my books, and I haven't spent a single rupee for this. A newspaper or magazine review will give your book credibility and worth. Do your best.

Tricks For Book Launches

WHILE MANY publishers and authors today question the effectiveness of the book launch—low attendance, limited impact, few book sales—it's a way for you to celebrate and create a buzz, especially if you're a new author. Let me warn you though: it's a lot of work and it can get overwhelming. Be prepared.

If you're having a book launch, have it in at least two places where you can draw crowds. You will need a venue: a bookstore, library, café or a cultural hub. Do not choose a location that is out of the way or unknown. If you're planning a launch in a big metropolis, plan in different parts of the city, so people are not inconvenienced. For example, an author in Mumbai will plan one book launch in South Mumbai and another in the suburbs, like Juhu or Andheri. Next you must find your chief guests; the ideal combination is of the celebrity (to draw in the crowds) and the intellectual (to draw out the substance). Fix a time and date, preferably mid-week after 6:30 pm or Sunday afternoons. Give yourself at least a three-week window to get organised. Try something more than a book reading and panel discussion; something offbeat that might entertain the guests: a musical performance, a 10-minute skit with a theme similar to your book, a gift giveaway, a theme-based pop quiz or party. As per the theme of your book—literary (nay!), commercial (yay!)—you can get creative and do a launch as an event, a party, on a boat, using props ... just about anything. Hell, Twinkle Khanna had a *Koffee With Karan* book launch with a duplicate set and a rapid-fire round. Amish Tripathi had a launch with drum circles and lathi-twirling. Remember, they had people working for them. You may not. So bite only as much as you can chew. Next, you must make the invite. At the venue you (along with the publisher and venue staff) must prepare for the book-signing table, the dais, the mikes, the chairs, the acoustics, the photographer (not compulsory; assign a friend or family member with a nice phone as the designated photographer) and other practical elements. The bookstore or venue, as well as your publisher, must send out the book launch invite to their database through their mailing list or newsletter, and create a buzz through flyers, banner standees and social media. Invite journalists, authors, book club enthusiasts, friends, colleagues, family, and anyone else you know. Emails and WhatsApp messages are the best options to send invites. Send a reminder a week before, two days prior and on the launch date. Plug the event all over social media. Be *besharam*. Make sure that there are enough copies of your book. Carry a working pen so you can sign the copies. Dress appropriately. Don't bore people by reading more than 5-10 minutes from your book. They'd rather talk to you and understand the person behind the book. Do a question and answer round. Don't forget to thank the bookstore owner and staff, and anyone else who helped you put the launch together. Thank the people who come to your launch. Despite work, despite kids, despite traffic, despite a hundred reasons not to, they're coming *only* for you. It's one of your biggest rewards as a writer. Enjoy yourself. This is your moment. You deserve it.

Your publisher should ideally help you find a book store or venue, make the invite, send out the invite to their mailing list, and arrange at least a hundred copies of your book. If they pitch in for tea and samosas, consider yourself lucky. If they agree to pay for wine and cheese, you, my friend, have arrived. Either way, see if you can arrange some tea or light snacks, nothing that will put a major dent on your pocket, but will help your readers feel better (who doesn't love *chai pe charcha*?). Don't expect lavish book tours. Publishers don't have budgets for those anymore. In fact, many of them have stopped book launches altogether. If you're a new author, you'll be lucky to have the publisher arrange a book launch in your hometown, and/or a big city like Mumbai or Delhi.

These days, since bookstores charge for book launches, celebrities ask for fat handouts, and publishers do not tend to sponsor five-star book tours or even one-star book launches, you can create your own book launch, offline or online. If you're travelling to a certain city for work or pleasure, contact a local bookstore, ask someone notable to attend, and have a book launch. It doesn't have to be big. It can even be a simple book reading or book signing. You can also do something that's totally free and almost effortless: a live Facebook/ Twitter/ Snapchat/ Instagram video, with a local celebrity, author, or prominent personality.

Another option: go on a virtual book tour on the blogosphere. Shortlist fifty book blogs that fit your genre and target audience. Pitch to them for a review. If you catch their interest, they can carry a book review, a book excerpt, an author interview, a guest post, a book giveaway campaign, or host a webinar for you. You can plan out these interactions over a few weeks or months. Some blogs charge an upfront fees, most don't. Most bloggers are passionate readers and staunch supporters of writers and writing; they'll be among your best friends as a new author. Be nice to them. They're in this for the love of books just as you are. If they like your book they'll promote it to the right audience and help you build a new readership base. Repay them by promoting these interactions online and participating in their blog even when you're not marketing your book.

One quick tip before we end this chapter. There will be people—friends, family and strangers—who will ask you for a free copy of your book. At some point, these insensitive requests will irk you. Learn how to respond in a way that is non-confrontational but firm. Tell the free-loader that you don't get free copies of your own book ... a book you have invested years of your life in ... and a book that will cost them less than a cup of (Starbucks) coffee. Would they appreciate it if you took a cut from their salary? Many people don't value the work that goes into the production of a book. Many people think that authors get an unlimited supply of free copies that are just lying around their house. Don't succumb to the demands of such entitled and tactless people. People should respect your work and you. Make that clear.

Book PR

THERE IS so much pressure on authors today to sell X number of copies within X number of weeks that book marketing has turned on its head from being virtually non-existent to being an industry in itself. Most books are bought in the first three weeks of their launch and their demand in the first month determines their demand going forward. While most literary authors have bowed out of this race—it's beneath their dignity and, frankly, bandwidth—book sales are the bread and butter for commercial fiction authors. The biggest mistake an author can make is to assume that her book will sell magically. The truth is that no matter what you write, if no one hears about your book, no one will buy your book. Remember, *jo dikhta hai wo bikta hai.*

So, get over this mind-block if you want your books to sell. I know it's irksome. I know you'd rather spend that time writing. But this is the way the world works today.

If you're not a *neta*, *abhineta*, celebrity, or Priyanka Chopra's dog, chances are that you do not have a massive following online or offline. Unlike our bestselling authors, you may also not have a marketing degree or an MBA. You may then wonder how you'll market your book. Where will you even begin? Your first instinct will be to look at your publisher for help. Forget about it. For a first-time author you'll be lucky if they even do a book launch for you. Until you have a proven track record of selling books, a publisher will not assign a big marketing budget for your book. A publisher will not heavily market your book because they will not make enough money off this endeavour. Therefore, and never forget this, the pressure to sell your book will fall almost squarely on your shoulders. So, what will you do?

First, accept the fact that in today's world you can't be just an author. To be successful, you also have to be a marketing genius. Think of who you are, how you want to be perceived, and how you can let readers engage with you. There is so much going on in the world today, so much that you can and should be involved with, having an opinion will help your social media profile immensely. Think of what you're passionate about outside of writing. If it's travelling, start conversations on the interesting places you've been to, the experiences you've had, tips for other travellers etc. If you love cooking, talk about recipes, share little tricks, put up—I dare say—food photographs etc. Be interesting. But don't jump on to a trend for the heck of it. I remember a lot of authors suddenly calling themselves feminists after the Merriam-Webster Dictionary named 'feminism' as the Word of the Year 2017. It was laughable. Don't put on an act. Be who you are. Be transparent. It's easy to spot a deceitful person.

In today's market if you want your book to sell you either have to be famous, be rich, be notorious, or be unique. Of course, a lot of our famous authors rake up controversies around the time of their new book launch, but don't forget to observe the way in which they doggedly engage with readers on social media day after day, through all the publishing deadlines and drafts. That requires some pluck and a lot of perseverance. Unfortunately, a lot people just don't have the stomach or time for it. Most of these people don't sell. If you want to sell, you will have to think of yourself as a brand. Even if the entire marketing department of your publisher is behind you or you've hired the best publicist in the country, you will still have to be a tenacious and bullheaded self-promoter. It's a lifelong commitment.

If you're dissatisfied with the marketing efforts of your publisher, your agent, and yourself, but you have deep pockets, then consider professional help to market your books. This is where public relation (PR) companies come in handy. While only a few specialise in book marketing, as it's not a big business for them, below is a list of those whom you can potentially approach: Book PR, BookBoys PR, Pink & White Consulting PR, Good Relations India, Paradigm Shift PR, FSB Associates, Weber Shandwick, Transcendent Strategy, Percept PR, El Sol Strategic Consultants, Think WhyNot and Mavcomm Consulting Pvt Ltd. Google and do your own research before approaching and deciding on someone. A PR company should not only help your book gain traction but also build your brand equity. They should get you reviews and blurbs, send your book to influencers, organise your book launches, get your name featured in lists, get you on guest blogs, get you bylines in prominent newspapers and news portals, along with helping you with tertiaries like movie deals, literature festival invites, speaker engagements etc. You will spend a few lakhs on them so use them well.

How Bestselling Authors Sell

LET'S TAKE a look at some of the marketing tools used by our nation's bestselling authors.

Mythology writer Amish Tripathi is among the highest selling authors in our country. It's not a surprise. Tripathi has all the ingredients that are required to produce a bestseller today: writing a good page-turner, understanding how marketing works (banker and MBA degree), executing a good marketing plan, and the discipline to both write and sell. This is despite the fact that his entry into the publishing world was nothing less than rough. Having found no publisher for his debut novel *The Immortals of Meluha*, Tripathi was forced to self-publish. While he did not expect to sell more than a few thousand copies, he took a chance, and came up with some ingenious marketing strategies. He pushed book marketing to where it had never gone before. Within a week of its launch his book was a bestseller and went on to become one of the highest selling books in the history of our country. Let's take a look at what Tripathi did.

Weeks before his debut novel was published, Tripathi persuaded bookstores to give away free sample copies of his book's first chapter. He made the first chapter available for free download on his website. Readers returned and bought the book in droves. He made a trailer film with a background score by percussionist Taufiq Qureshi, uploaded it on YouTube, and shared it extensively on Facebook and Twitter. It was a hit.

When Tripathi went to a new city or town he made it a point to visit as many bookstores as he could. He is rumoured to know the name of every bookstore manager. He made presentations about his book to big retail chains, smaller retailers, and local distributors. Every fortnight Tripathi mailed various stakeholders new statistics for his books—how much had sold, where, how fast, and what new initiatives he was planning. He followed up with distributors to ensure that his book reached every tempted reader. One can only imagine the love that book retailers and distributors felt for Tripathi.

After the success of his first two books, Tripathi understood who his target market was. He knew that his readers went to movie halls and watched television. So, for his next book *The Oath Of The Vayuputras*, he made an impactful book trailer for these mediums. Such high production quality and visual effects for a book trailer had never been seen in India before. The book was a runaway hit.

Tripathi also gave the concept of the book launch a fillip and took it to another level. According to *Hindustan Times*, he made presentations about his book to big retail chains, smaller retailers, and local distributors. This is what happened at his book's 2013 Mumbai launch: "An hour before the 10pm launch, fans had already lined up outside, chanting 'Har Har Mahadev!' Some were dressed as characters from the series; others sported tattoos featuring artwork from the books. There were bouncers for crowd control, numbered tokens to prevent queue jumping and MCs to entertain everyone. Artists painted Shiva body art for obliging fans. Dancers performed to music especially created for the book. It was Indian publishing's biggest party."

The ingenuity didn't stop at the build-up, it continued even after the mega-success of the book. Read what was further written: "At a five-star hotel ... guests drank milky 'somrass' out of earthen cups, little dumroos at every table allowed for a different kind of audience applause, buffet items were named to reflect characters and locations in the novels, and everyone went home with a souvenir – a scroll bearing the Pashupati seal that features prominently in the books. The only thing missing, as someone cheekily announced over the speakers that evening, was a chillum of hashish."

Tripathi then threw a small party where, in a mini Oscar-style ceremony, individual trophies were given to the photographer, cinematographer, PR team, advertising people, and the promotions team. He didn't forget to say 'thank you'.

Tripathi did what other authors generally don't. He followed neither industry standard nor protocol. He pushed the envelope. He took a chance on himself. He kept his eyes on the trees and the forest—the big guns and the little guys. He put in as much effort, if not more, in selling his books as he did in writing them. This is not everyone's cup of tea—one can only imagine the amount of hard work and meticulous planning that must have gone in to market the books. Phew!

But look at the results: the Shiva trilogy series ended up selling 2 million copies and counting, with retail sales clocking in tens of crores. Tripathi quit his job and became a full-time writer, making headlines for getting paid an unheard of Rs 5 crore for his next mythology series. And it all came down to being impressively disciplined when it came to marketing his books. Worth it? You decide.

The other mega-bestselling author, known to be the biggest selling English language novelist in India's history, is Chetan Bhagat. The author's journey also got off to a less than glamorous start. Major publishers rejected his debut book *Five Point Someone*. He could've retreated quietly to the corners of his unrealised dreams; instead he fought back by tweaking the way he was pitching.

Five Point Someone sold more than a million copies.

What contributed to his success? To begin with, Bhagat was clear about whom he was writing for: the aspirational middle class for whom English was a second language, but who wanted to be seen holding an English-language book. He was clear about the market that he was selling to: not the market for high literature that existed in India, but the market for lowbrow books that did not exist before he created it. That's where the easy money was. He was also clear about his personal goals: he wanted to be the bestselling writer, but not the best writer, at a time when this kind of thought was an anomaly. It wouldn't be wrong to say that Bhagat was a change agent who had the foresight to know what India wanted to read and how deep India's readership base was.

For his other books Bhagat adopted these marketing strategies. He sold T-shirts featuring quotes from his books. Readers could get a discount on his books if they followed him on Facebook. He allowed readers access to the first chapter of his book *The 3 Mistakes Of My Life* for free. After that, they could read the rest of his book only if they send the book link to three friends. He wrote for English and Hindi newspapers; Hindi because his target audience read regional newspapers. He hosted TV shows. He delivered talks. His publisher wrapped entire local train coaches with his book covers and conducted contests where winners got a chance to meet the author. Bhagat's massive reach came about as his books were converted to Bollywood movies, and most went on to become hits. He was everywhere. Bhagat knew how to stay in the news. He was aware that there was no such thing as bad publicity. He was also unafraid of coming across as pompous, often times opening his books by inserting himself in the story, further propagating the Chetan Bhagat brand. Through all this, Bhagat maintained that his marketing spends were zero. When Flipkart gave him a front-page ad for the launch of one of his books, he said the company paid for it in exchange for exclusivity.

Bhagat's success has come despite drawing flak from the literary circles and being dismissed as an 'unthinker' writing 'non-novels'. While many may criticise him for putting more effort into his marketing plan than writing his books, the fact is that Bhagat sells more than a daily newspaper in a city! He has sold over a million copies each of the books he's written. He has changed the way India reads and, in many ways, the way India writes. This is not something to disregard.

He's also one of the only Indian authors to make crores from his books. Writes one publication, "Bhagat's Revolution 2020 has sold 1.5 million copies, with 1 million copies selling within 100 days. Rupa has set a target of 2 million copies for his next book. At 140 each, and royalty varying from 10-15% for the author, if all 2 million copies are sold, it would mean a neat take-home of more than 4 crore for Chetan. Taking all his five books into account, Bhagat has already made approximately over 15 crore." Bhagat's movie deals have also scored him lakhs. For example, his book *2 States* was allegedly sold as a film for around Rs 65 lakh.

Some of our other bestselling writers have also devised innovative ways and unique strategies to sell their books. Romance author Ravinder Singh launched a song by singer Shaan to promote his book *Like It Happened Yesterday*. Savi Sharma posted inspirational quotes on the Facebook page of her debut novel *Everyone Has A Love Story*, packaging her book as 'inspirational romance'. Among many unique social media campaigns and brand tie-ins, Durjoy Datta splashed his engagement and marriage photos all over social media and the tabloids, further cementing himself as the brand ambassador of romance. Thriller writer Ravi Subramanian made the reader an important stakeholder in the marketing process by asking readers to decide the ending to his books, devising a 'Litcoin' Facebook game for his book *If God Was a Gamer*, tying up with Costa Coffee to give free bookmarks, and hosting several events centered around 'meet the author'. Shobhaa De launched a blog and YouTube 'sting operation' for the protagonist of her novel *Sethji* using a campaign *Who is Sethji?* All successful mass-market authors engage with their readers on a daily basis; they respond to every tweet, every Insta comment, and every Facebook message. That takes a lot of work!

Of course, if only well-sold books and not well-written books are published, the publishing industry stands to lose bibliodiversity and become irrelevant. In an ideal world commercial fiction authors would sell literary fiction books, and we would all be happy.

Authors writing great books often fall by the wayside because they don't know how to promote themselves or don't believe in the concept. Many believe that their book will take its own journey after it's been published—bestseller or not. They believe in what the Bhagavad Gita says, "Do an action not for its consequences or rewards, but out of devotion to the act itself." While, this is a romantic notion to hang on to, the fact is that as an author you've spent years working on a book. If you have to spend another month or four to heavily promote your book, then you must at least consider it. I say this so that readers become aware that there are also good books out there, for our country needs to start reading the best authors and not just the bestselling ones.

CHAPTER FOUR
ESSAYS

A Writer's Secrets: Jeffrey Archer

I AM often asked the secret to writing a bestseller. There is no secret. Writing is hard work, and getting published is harder still. I'm now writing my new novel, and it's just as tough a challenge today, as when I wrote *Kane and Abel* nearly 40 years ago. Nevertheless, although I believe that the ability to tell a story is a God-given gift, if you have a passion to write then don't give up. I'm happy to share a few of my tips.

1. **Make time:** Decide when you're going to write. Don't be casual and only do it as and when it fits in with your social life. Don't think you can write a novel after you've done a hard day's work, it's insulting to those professional novelists who spend their time doing nothing else.

2. **Be disciplined:** For example, I write from 6-8am, 10-12, 2-4pm, 6-8pm. I keep that routine up for 40-50 days and handwrite every word. I then take a break and go back to it again a month later.

3. **Write what you know:** At least when you start out. Don't do vampires, wizards or ghosts just because they're in fashion. Jane Austen wrote about family life in a small village and gave us six of the greatest novels ever written.

4. **Get some fresh air:** I go for two long walks between sessions, for two reasons, physical and mental. The plot will buzz around in your mind while you are walking, continually churning over, which it can't be while you're actually writing.

5. **Do several drafts:** Do not imagine that the first draft of your book is the one that will be published. My novel, *Heads You Win*, was 14 drafts and took approximately 1000 hours.

6. **Be flexible:** If you think of something better half-way through the writing process, don't be frightened to go back and incorporate it, or even change the story completely, as I did in my latest book.

7. **Seek opinions from professionals:** When you want an opinion on what you consider the finished script, seek it from a professional editor, an agent or someone you don't know, through a third party. Do not seek an opinion from your wife, husband, partner, or close friend. They will lie.

8. **Read the greats:** There is no substitute for reading great novelists, and instead of just enjoying their craft, think carefully about how they've achieved it? Do they spend pages on description, do they move the story on quickly, how do they make you turn the page? It's all there in front of you if you look carefully, so at least when you try to do it, you have analysed how successful authors have managed it in the past.

9. **Stay fit:** If the body is a physical wreck—too much drinking, smoking, late nights—how can you expect the written word to be anything less than drunken, useless and tired?

10. **Don't give up:** My first novel, *Not a Penny, Not a Penny Less*, was turned down by 14 publishers, ended up with an advance of £3,000 and on first printing took a year to sell 3,000 copies. It is still extremely rare for a first book to be a bestseller, and even rarer to be published by the first person who reads it.

Jeffrey Archer has topped the bestseller lists around the world, with sales of over 275 million copies in 97 countries and more than 37 languages. He is the only author ever to have been a number one bestseller in fiction (nineteen times), short stories (four times) and non-fiction (The Prison Diaries). Jeffrey has served five years in the House of Commons and twenty-six years as a Member of the House of Lords.

Writing Tips: Twinkle Khanna

READ EVERYTHING you can get your hands on: Programme your mind to read all the time and everywhere—even in the bathroom, skim through the lines printed on the back of shampoo bottles and sanitary napkin packets.

Eat carbohydrates: All these protein diets may help you twirl prettily in a size-2 dress but if you want your mind to take a few marvelous leaps then you have to give it the food it needs.

Live in the world of probabilities: Examine things with a magnifying glass made up only of what-ifs.

Find a tolerant family: These kind folk must accept the fact that you may sit at your desk for hours at a time while spouting vague excuses like 'I will come out later, it's too hot' or 'Don't come close, there are insects on my desk!'

Walk, run, cycle: When you live inside your head for such long periods of time, you have to open the windows, air it out a bit, let sunlight stream into all the dark and dusty corners of your mind.

Relish being an oddball: Well-behaved, well-adjusted people are hopeless storytellers and, honestly, terribly boring.

This article was originally published in Vogue (December 2016) and on Vogue.in (https://www.vogue.in/content/eat-carbohydrates-writing-tips-twinkle-khanna/). Published with permission.

Twinkle Khanna is an author, newspaper columnist, film producer, former film actress and interior designer. Her first book Mrs Funnybones sold over one hundred thousand copies, making her India's highest-selling female writer of 2015, and winning her the Crossword Book Award 2016. She repeated the success with her second book, The Legend of Lakshmi Prasad, which also went on to sell over 100,000 copies by August 2017.

What It Takes To Be A Writer: Preeti Shenoy

MOST RUNNERS speak of a 'runner's high'—that endorphin rush you feel when you've been involved in strenuous activity, leading to a feeling of euphoria and happiness. Yesterday, I hit a writer's high. It was something I have never experienced before. I wrote 8300 words in a single day. That is the highest ever number of words I have written in a single day, in my entire writing career.

I patted myself on the back.

And when a friend messaged to ask how the writing was going, I replied, 'Super, I hit a writer's high today. This is the highest number of words I have written in a single day in my entire life.'

'Wow. Keep rocking!' he typed back.

But I don't think he understood why it meant a great deal to me.

Writing a book is a lot of work really. You have to think of a story (a completely original one which no one has done before, which by itself is a mammoth task), a plot, characters (they have to be likeable, believable, and people who you can relate to), dialogues, what happens to them. You have to write coherently. But more than anything, you have to discipline yourself to sit at the computer all by yourself and type out word after word after word. Day after day after day.

It is a L.O.N.E.L.Y. profession. You have to be involved with people and interested in them and understand them, empathize with them, yet be strangely detached, to be able to write.

There is no one really to check your progress and nobody you are accountable to. So that makes it that much more harder. You can take a year, two years, even five years to finish a book. It is so entirely up to you and you alone. I have my own ways of pushing myself. Sometimes I compete with fellow authors who are working on a book. We ping each other at the end of the day and ask, 'WC?' (WC stands for word count. There is great joy in typing 2,300 or 3,200 or whatever the number of words one has written. A sense of satisfaction of a day well spent.)

Sometimes I tell a friend (whom I am dying to meet) that I will go out with them only when I hit 'x' number of words. Then they keep checking as to how many words I have written so that we can go out. I report my progress to my children and spouse and the househelp, as well as my dog. They are the only ones who actually care about my word count. Or rather, they are the only ones who will listen to me. (Oh, and that friend too who I promise to go out with, on completing 'x' words.)

Yesterday I crossed 60,000 words of the book I am working on. (Which was when I hit the writer's high.)

'Oh, so does that mean the book will be out soon?' asked the friend.

'No! The real work starts now!' I replied.

Most people do not know that once a manuscript is complete, and a publisher is chosen, it takes a minimum of 4-6 months for the book to be out. The manuscript goes through the first revision. The structural changes, if any, are suggested to the author. The author then incorporates the changes or convinces the editor about why the changes should not happen. Then begins the proofreading. The first round is done and the manuscript comes back to the author. Generally it looks like a war-field, with all the corrections looking like blood-wounds. I winced when it first came. I kid you not. Then the corrections are made and sent back. Each coma, each full stop, each word, is examined over and over. Then the second round of proofreading happens.

Then the third. Sometimes the fourth and fifth. (I have proofread till the words begin blurring and I fall asleep in front of my laptop.)

We squabble about fonts. About an exclamation mark. About a word repeated. Every single detail counts. Then the cover. And the book title. And the acknowledgements. And the chapter titles. And how it should all appear in the final version. And finally it is a BIG moment when the book gets an okay and goes for printing. For my last book, up to the last moment, we were making changes. It is something like a rocket-blast off— the frantic holding-of-breath till it takes off.

The tension doesn't end there.

When you finally hold the book in your hands (the much coveted author copies), it is truly a moment that makes me weep. Every single time. No matter how many books you have written, it is still the same.

Welcome to the writer's world.

It is a lonely place, a crazy place, a place which makes you hurtle down into depths of despair when you can't get those words out, but at the same time, a place which makes you soar higher than even the heavens when things go right.

This piece first appeared in *Love A Little Stronger*, by Preeti Shenoy. Published with permission.

Preeti Shenoy, among the top five highest selling authors in India, is also on the Forbes longlist of the most influential celebrities in India. She is the highest selling woman writer in India. Her work has been translated to many languages. India Today has named her as being unique for being the only woman in the bestselling league.

She has been awarded the 'Indian of the Year' award (2017) by Brands Academy for her contribution to literature. She has also received the Academia award for Business Excellence by the New Delhi Institute of Management. She has a very popular blog and also writes a weekly column in The Financial Chronicle.

Why You Should Write: Rashmi Bansal

MANY BUDDING authors in India send me their manuscripts. I am always surprised to see how many of these are written by MBA graduates.

The first possibility that comes to mind is that there's an artist hidden in each one of us. But due to the pursuit of 'safe careers', very few are willing to take a risk and pursue artistic professions. It is only when they have settled down, got the degree, the designation and the monthly paycheck, that the urge to 'be creative' surfaces.

But the majority of these manuscripts are lifeless. I mean, when you read the words, you don't *feel* a thing. After a few pages you don't even want to read further.

So what goes wrong? Clearly, the author has put in time and effort. And has intellectual capacity. The trouble is that the book is written MBA-style—all from the head, not from the heart. Hence, the characters are flat and uni-dimensional. The plot is predictable. The language is correct but stiff, and no fun to read.

In short, there is no 'flow' in the writing. And this is because the author has heavily relied on the Left Brain. An obedient slave and faithful servant, the left-brain is logical, rational and extremely useful when you wish to clear an entrance exam or create a complicated spreadsheet.

But, it is an impediment if you want to do anything in the realm of art.

Art is an expression of one's innermost being. At the same time it is a reminder of the tiny, insignificant human self. Singers and dancers perform, writers and painters create. Yes, the paintbrush is moving, the fingers are typing but the artist knows, it's not just 'me'. I am an instrument, through which thoughts and ideas are flowing. I am connected to a Higher Source.

This is why creative people often appear to be 'lost' in themselves, in that Other Dimension where your 'book' is waiting to be found. Robert Louis Stevenson (Treasure Island) conceived entire novels through dreams. Elizabeth Gilbert (Eat, Pray, Love) gave a brillant TED talk in which she argued that creativity is divinely inspired. Amish Tripathi says that writing his books is like a 'joyful ride'. Quoting from an interview he gave to *The Economic Times*: "The only thing I had to do was to listen to music, which (matched) the mood of the moment that I am writing in ... and somehow the story would just start flowing ... there wasn't any logic to it. Sometimes I would write chapter 25, the next day I would write chapter five ... I learned not to question it and would write just what came to me. I first wrote summaries of the three books and then I started expanding them into the books."

I'm not saying that if *you* switch on your favourite music a bestseller will just flow out of your pen. But at some point, it can, if you learn to access the power of your sub-conscious mind.

The other qualities that I believe make for success are:

1. Being pigheaded (believing in your story and way of writing when no one else will)
2. Being ahead of your time (what you've written has not been seen or done before)
3. Being I-don't-give-a-damn (I started writing for fun, not to make serious money or a big career)

So, my final bit of advice is: do not write with 'goals' in mind. Do not write for the 'audience'. There is one reason—and only one reason—why you should be writing.

Because there's a song in your soul, waiting to be sung.

Rashmi Bansal is a best-selling non-fiction writer. She has published 9 books on entrepreneurship.

How To Find A Good Story: Kunal Basu

IF YOU'RE looking to write a story, you need to start practicing the art of finding one. Every story begins with something—either an idea, the whiff of a plot, sketch of a character, or an event—that demands to be written. To explore this process of how you might go about finding stories to tell, here are some tips:

Be Inspired: My inspiration to tell stories comes from my childhood. My mother was a well-known novelist in Bengal, while my father was a publisher. We discussed books in our house, held debates on literature, and had many famous writers visit. At that age getting a book as a present was more important to me than getting toys, and I am yet to get over the romance of books.

Keep A Story-Making Mind: From where does a novelist get stories? This is a difficult question to answer. Stories first appear in the mind. Therefore, one must sustain a story-making mind. This means that you must have a mind that is receptive to stories by being neither overly judgmental nor too analytical. Don't rush into forming an opinion of a person or situation. Story making is like daydreaming. What's important is to allow your mind to dream and absorb, and to go where your mind takes you.

Find A Source: While I have no fixed destination to find stories, there are three sources that tend to work for me. These are:

1. **Designed Experiences:** While one cannot find stories on demand, I find travel to be an important source, since you don't know what will transpire or whom you'll meet. Travel means going out of one's comfort zone and encountering people, experiences and vocations that one would normally never encounter. I'm an intrepid travel and two of my novels and several short stories have come out of my travels.

2. **Episodic Memory:** You must mine your own memory. Recall small episodes that you may have considered minor or those that were hidden beneath major experiences. For example, read letters you've written from twenty years ago or dig out old photographs. Ask questions like: What was I like when I was 17? Who were my friends and enemies? What were my dreams?

3. **Be A Voyeur:** Odd as this sounds, you must eavesdrop on people's conversations. A story about an Indian man and his Japanese wife ("The Japanese Wife") I wrote came out of a conversation I eavesdropped on while on a ferryboat. The impulse for story-making often comes from overhearing the conversations of strangers. Today I see young people on trains, buses and airports with their earphones plugged in. This way you're shutting out the life that's happening spontaneously around you.

Tap Into The Unfamiliar: Many aspiring authors attend creative writing programs where they're told to write what they know i.e. if you know your neighbourhood well, then write about that. Therefore, many early works of writers are often autobiographical in nature. While it's fine for others to find stories in familiar worlds, I seek stories within the unfamiliar. For me the familiar world is interesting but not interesting enough. I seek out aspects of life that are beyond my reach. The excitement of story-making for me is to dive into an unknown world.

It is important therefore, to keep my eyes and ears open. When I'm in India, I don't own a car on purpose, and normally walk or take a taxi. I walk around aimlessly during the night and day. Once when I was walking down a lane in Kolkata, I found a bunch of well-dressed men on their motorcycles hanging outside hotels where tourists stay. I befriended a juice-stall owner who told me that these men were male prostitutes who would provide drugs and sex to their clients. A world started opening up inside my mind. Curious, I put myself in their path and went to places they hung out to see what happens in their life. A story was born. If I hadn't been inquisitive I would've never known this aspect of the city.

Funnel Ideas: Every good story starts with a good idea. Story ideas are all around us. How can a writer know which idea to pursue and which to dispense? A story doesn't appear fully formed but as fragments which blend into your imagination. So which one should you pick? I pick a story where my heart engages, the one that I feel emotionally drawn to. If I don't see myself in a story, even if it's a good one, then it's better left alone for someone else to tell. You must feel a powerful connect with a story. Since you are likely to spend quite a few months (years even!) with a novel, you have to be emotionally invested in it. So the question I ask is: Would the story keep me awake at night?

Block Writer's Block: I've written 10 books in 18 years. Since I go from book to book the notion of a writer's block is lost to me. But some days you write better than others. Sometimes you struggle. What do I do then? I'm also an artist. When the novel is stuck in my mind, I'll go from my writing desk to my easel. I'll spend a day or two painting, and when I come back to my writing desk miraculously that block opens up. I stay with creativity but shift courses.

Write With Arrogance: When you're writing you should not seek feedback from a friend or family member or agent or publisher. Firstly, not any one view is correct or right. Secondly, what really helps writing is having a small touch of arrogance, not huge, but small. You need to be a master of what you are creating. To work it out in your mind you must know the way forward instead of seeking opinion. You must keep your mind unpolluted. Once the book is finished then readers are entitled to their opinion. Remember, writing is not a democratic process but an autocratic one.

Kunal Basu was born in Kolkata and educated in India and the USA. He is the author of five critically acclaimed novels, The Opium Clerk; The Miniaturist; Racists; The Yellow Emperor's Cure and Kalkatta He has also written a collection of short stories, The Japanese Wife, of which the title story has been made into an award-winning film. He has published three Bengali novels. His works have been translated into several languages and nominated for prestigious awards. Basu has worked as a filmmaker, actor, and professor—at McGill University, and most recently at the University of Oxford. He lives in Oxford and Kolkata.

Finding Your Point Of View: Manil Suri

NOVELISTS WILL often display a predilection for a particular narrative point of view. Some seem to favor the strength and immediacy of a first-person "I." Others like the intimacy of a second-person "you." Most popular, perhaps, is the objectivity of the third-person "he/she/they." Which option is best?

For my first novel, the choice was almost automatic. The book sprang from images I'd actually seen: a man named Vishnu dying on the steps of my parents' apartment building in Mumbai, a cup of tea someone had left lying untouched next to his body.

I knew the story would be about how the building's (fictional) residents dealt with this, that I'd simply be an unseen observer. Third-person offered a natural vehicle to capture the motives and interactions of the large cast of characters. Referring to them formally by their last names ("Mrs. Jaiswal was cheating again, and as usual, there was nothing Mrs. Pathak could do about it") underscored the humor in the proceedings. I considered switching to first person for Vishnu himself, to make his segments distinct, more ethereal for the reader. But this made him the de facto narrator of the story, ruining the "fly on the wall" effect I wanted. I solved the problem by writing Vishnu's pieces in the present tense, with the rest in the past.

The second novel took some cogitation—Meera, the heroine, resisted all my efforts to capture her voice. When she finally began speaking, it was not to me, but to her infant son Ashvin—whom she was breast-feeding. "Every time I touch you, every time I kiss you, every time I offer you my body."

That's when I realized I had entered the uncharted (for me) territory of second-person—Meera would address the book to her son, as an account, an exculpation, of their life together. This second-person "world of two" neatly closed off everyone else, emphasizing that Ashvin was the focal point of Meera's life, in whom she finds, and loses, herself.

At first, my editor wondered if it might be too claustrophobic; create too much distance between the reader and the characters. But I convinced her that Meera's "you" also encompasses readers—who are able to imagine themselves not just in Meera's place but also her son's. ("Do you know how innocent you look, how helpless, as I guide the nipple towards your mouth?")

With my third novel, "The City of Devi," it seemed natural to return to second-person, in which my lovelorn heroine Sarita could address her missing husband Karun, whom she sets out to find in the desolate streets of war-ravaged Mumbai. A few hundred pages later, I realized how my choice had boxed me in: second-person is woefully ill-suited for describing action, which this novel cried out for.

So I shifted gears into first-person. To my alarm, long tracts of meditative material, representing months of toil, suddenly began falling away. Plotlines were transformed, and the novel revealed its secret "thriller" aspirations, hidden within all along. Most exhilaratingly, a revamped second narrator named Jaz was born. His cocky voice ("Sex was my true calling, my raison d'être—as guilt-free as yoghurt, as natural as rain") gave the novel a fearless new exuberance. In an interesting twist, Jaz often refers to himself ironically in the third person.

In my latest novel, "The Godfather of Numbers," I'm using *all* three choices. The eponymous narrator explains the origins of mathematics to "you," the reader, but also talks in the first person about himself. And being omniscient, he relates what happens to other characters in the third person. Which just goes to show that each novel has its own optimal match. Just be prepared to switch if a choice proves incorrect!

— *Originally published (in modified form) in The Wall Street Journal, February 9th 2013*

Manil Suri was born in Mumbai and moved to the US when he was 20-years-old. He has a Ph.D. in Applied Mathematics from Carnegie-Mellon University and is now a Professor at the University of Maryland Baltimore County; his area of research is Finite Element Analysis. Suri received a Guggenheim Fellowship in 2004. Suri is the author of a trilogy, The Death of Vishnu, The Age of Shiva, and The City of Devi. He is now working on a book about mathematics for non-mathematicians, The M Word.

Unleash Your Creativity:
Namita Gokhale

AT A time when the act of writing has become almost synonymous with promoting the cultivated persona of the author and with relentless publicity for the book object, I would like to remind myself and other writers of why we sit in solitude, to search the right word, to construct a story, to build a narrative. This may be counterintuitive in our frenetic social media driven world, but in my view, it is to share the empathy of other lives, as well as to understand ourselves, and to grow and evolve in the process.

Creativity is the capacity for rediscovering joy, finding new connectivities, of dreaming and imagining, of making, crafting and innovating in any and every aspect of one's life. Albert Einstein is quoted as saying, "Creativity is intelligence having fun". He also provocatively stated that, "Creativity is the residue of time wasted." I tend to agree. Personally, in my creative endeavors, when I try too hard, nothing significant happens. When I let go and surrender to the flow of thoughts, I am productive, effective and efficient.

Let us also remember what Steve Jobs said: "Creativity is just connecting things. When you ask creative people how they did something, they feel a little guilty because they didn't really do it. That's because they were able to connect experiences they have had and synthesize new things. And the reason they were able to do that was that they've had more experiences, or they've thought more about their experiences than other people."

In Steve Jobs' perspective, imagination can indeed take the place of experience. Effective writing combines the dreaming mind, with grounded understanding and experience; this experience often comes from wide and eclectic reading.

Another rule. Fear and creativity cannot co-exist. Creativity demands courage. Challenges stimulate creativity. If we are continuously self-censoring, we cannot give play to our imagination and write effectively.

What is called 'Third Space Thinking' has been described as involving the following:

#Empathy and Creativity
#Intellectual Curiosity
#Adaptability and Flexibility
#Innovation

Quality writing also requires daily discipline and focus. It has to become part of the rhythm of one's life. All writers have different rhythms in which they write. I find I take time to settle down and enter the zone. It is rather like a dog settling into the grass, a movement ingrained into even domesticated animals as they circle a space to find a spot. Many other writers I know have a pet tic, a habit of distracted and familiar movements, thoughts to access the subconscious mind and to cross over to a parallel world.

Many writers suffer blockages, when they cannot articulate and write all they want to. In my experience, this is often because they have not processed their material enough, or sometimes processed it too much. In writing, as in life, timing is everything, as are the silences between words, the introspection and meditation, as well as the fire of spontaneity. The courage as well as the caution, obedience as well as disobedience, discipline as well as rebellion, all these contradictions nurture creativity.

Namita Gokhale is a well-renowned writer, publisher and festival director. She is the author of fifteen books including nine works of fiction.

How To Create A Masterpiece:
Vikas Swarup

AS A writer I am often asked, how do you get your ideas? And it is a difficult question for me to answer because the process through which ideas come into a writer's head is a mysterious one. Nevertheless, I tried to decode it and I came up with what I call the 3 Cs.

So how does the creative process actually begin?

I think the first step to tapping the source of creativity that lies in all of us, is curiosity, the first C.

Apples had been falling on people's heads for centuries, but why did it take a Newton to discover the theory of gravity? Because Newton was curious. As William Hazzlitt put it, "Millions saw the apple fall, but Newton was the one who asked why!"

If the mind is like a muscle, then it needs to be exercised regularly and there is no better mental exercise than curiosity. Curiosity is actively exploring your environment, asking questions.

When we are curious, we see things differently; we use our powers of observation more fully. A hungry mind is a prerequisite for successful innovation. When the mind is curious, new ideas can come from anywhere, from an overheard conversation or a serendipitous discovery, from a disturbing nightmare or a melodious tune, from a book, a newspaper, even an interesting looking rock.

To take my own example, the inspiration for my first novel *Q&A* came from a news report I had read in 1999 about a project called 'Hole in the Wall'. In that project a group of computer scientists working at the NIIT campus in Delhi carved a hole in the wall that adjoined the Kalkaji slum and put up for use a freely accessible computer. This computer proved to be an instant hit among the slum dwellers, especially the children. And the scientists discovered that these slum children started using that computer entirely on their own, without any teachers, without having had any formal education. And I thought, if a slum kid can use a computer, he can also participate in a brain quiz, and win. So I juxtaposed these two themes—of a game show, and of a contestant who has had no formal education, who has 'street knowledge' as opposed to 'book knowledge'. That is how *Q&A/Slumdog Millionaire* was born.

So, real life can be a source of endless inspiration. I always say that just reading one day's newspaper in India can give me ideas for four or five different plots. But the best inspiration for a writer is most often, other writers. You need not know these writers personally, you should know them through their works. I always used to be a voracious reader. I think this was one of the advantages of growing up in a pre-internet, pre-cable TV era that there were no other distractions and, for most people, the only pass time was reading. So I read a lot and it was only through this process of reading that I came to appreciate what good writing meant. And by learning from the craft of these writers, I was able to search for my own voice, my own style.

The second C is Confidence. Confidence is equally important, because creativity is about taking risks. You don't know if the idea you have in your head is an idea that will appeal to other people as well.

Everyone in India seems to have a grandmother's story. But your grandmother's story may not be of great interest to people outside your immediate family. So if you think it has some universal message, which is relevant to society, then you need to take the risk and find out. A culture of risk aversion is not good for creativity. So try and fail, but don't fail to try.

In my last book *The Accidental Apprentice*, I decided to write in the voice of a female protagonist called Sapna Sinha. It was difficult at first. I had to imagine the world from the eyes of a 23-year-old salesgirl who works in an electronic boutique in Connaught Place. Every Friday she goes to the Hanuman Temple on Baba Kharak Singh Marg to pray. And one day she is accosted by an elderly billionaire who makes her the most amazing offer you can imagine: I want to make you the CEO of my ten billion dollar company, provided you pass seven tests from the textbook of life. The novel begins with the line: *In life you never get what you deserve, you get what you negotiate*. The same holds true for writing. You have to have the confidence to negotiate your writing on your own terms.

But for every book that becomes a bestseller, there are thousands in which readers don't make it past the second or third chapter. And that is why testing becomes crucial. Get frank advice from someone who has no stake in promoting you to realize the true worth of what you've created.

The last thing you need is a computer, the third C, for the research. Research is important to help you create an authentic backdrop, especially when you are writing about subjects of which you have no personal knowledge. I thanked Google in my first book for making research so much faster. And, in my second novel *Six Suspects*, I even had a character called Larry Page, the founder of Google.

Today, thanks to the information revolution, a poor, young girl with an Internet enabled cell-phone has as much knowledge at her disposal as a millionaire with ten thousand books in his library. And it is this democratization of technology that will unleash the creativity of a billion Indians.

So go ahead and create your masterpiece.

Vikas Swarup is an Indian diplomat and writer. He has written three novels—Q&A, which was converted into the multiple Oscar-winning film Slumdog Millionaire, Six Suspects and The Accidental Apprentice. His books have been translated into more than 40 international languages.

How To Write Bestsellers For Four Decades: Shobhaa De

LET'S TALK turkey: The world's first 'bestseller' was The Bible. It remains a top seller even today. Wonder which canny marketing team marketed and sold it after its first print run? The Bible outsells most commercial books globally. Over centuries, readers have been hooked to this one religious book, which comes with a single absorbing tagline: God created Adam and Eve. Sheer brilliance. Try topping it. Go on ... give it a go.

Bestsellers are born naturally, not constructed in a petri dish. It is not possible to 'predict' the birth of a best seller, or even guess its sex. It comes with its own DNA. And even the world's savviest, canniest analyst cannot clone it.

During my long experience as a published author and publisher, I can only pass on this bit of useless advice: Write from your heart .... lungs ... kidneys ... even bladder. Do not waste a moment worrying about your precious book's fate. It is not in your hands. Remember: it is not in your publisher's hands, either. There is just one pair of hands that matters—the readers. You, as an author, can never know your reader. You may think you do. But books have an uncanny way of meandering into hands whose existence you are not even aware of. Respect the mind of that anonymous reader. The one who has bought YOUR book over millions of other books. Your reader is your God.

Pay zero attention to critics. Most don't have the guts to write their own book. Books need guts. Of course, there are critics and critics. Do share glasses of your favourite wine with them. But they will still loathe you. The best critic is just you. Only you. If you love your book, others may love it, too. If you display diffidence, give in to uncertainty, you are dead. Never apologise for your thoughts and words. Own them. Take criticism on the chin. And start your new book instantly.

Don't treat your book like a premature baby. Do not molly coddle. Or even potty train. Like kids say, "Shit happens!" Let it happen. Books are tougher than you think. They survive! Some even thrive. Their good health is not your problem, after they leave the womb. They belong to everyone. Books, like street urchins, manage to get ahead and survive against terrible odds. That is the real kick, my dear—watching your urchin conquer the world.

Writing a book is a little like making tender love to yourself. You really don't need an extra pair of hands. Or two brains. You know your G-Spot. Just get there and get on with the job. Do you count orgasms? Or create spreadsheets for your matings? You just go ahead and make love, right? So ... when in doubt, simply get between those sheets, or inside a bathtub and do what you have to. Think of your book as a lover. A sensitive lover. Not a demanding beast. The sensual act of writing a book and making ardent love are a lot alike. Both provide unimaginable pleasure and create beautiful memories. What? You don't like sex? Why are you a writer? Open a candy store and sell bon bons. Leave bon mots to others.

Shobhaa De is one of India's best-known novelists and columnists. She has written 20 books, most of which have become bestsellers. The former editor of magazines like Stardust, Society and Celebrity, Shobhaa has been a model and scriptwriter.

How The Agent Works With The Publisher And Author:
Sherna Khambatta

MANY PEOPLE ask me what I do as a literary agent and if I sit around reading books all day? It must be the best job in the world, especially if you're a book lover! Well, they are partly right and partly wrong. I do have the privilege of reading a lot of manuscripts that turn into books, and being a passionate bibliophile is the primary reason I became an agent, but it also gives me immense joy to see a manuscript evolve into a book in a store.

If you want a book to be published by a traditional publisher a literary agent acts like the first filter to that work. So what is it that my job as an agent entails?

Step 1: A writer sends me a synopsis and sample chapters of the work. My preference is non-fiction work.

Step 2: I ask for the full manuscript.

Step 3: Only if I am confident that I can represent the given work do I offer the author representation. If a work is rejected I do not explain why since that would be a full-time job in itself!

Step 4: Once we have a contract signed, the author and I work on the text. We polish it up, and re-read it umpteen times to check if there are any typos and if the work reads well.

Once the author and I are both confident that it is the best version of the manuscript, I start sending it out to various editors. An agent keeps track of what editors are looking for, the best imprint, and the best publishing house for the given work. I work both with Indian publishers as well as those abroad. I share a list of the publishers with the author, and as rejections or interests come in I share the same immediately.

Step 5: Once the manuscript has been sent out and an editor is interested in it, I follow up with them and send them the rest of the manuscript, if they request it. I'd also like to mention here that until this point I don't get paid for all the work that's been done! Since we only receive income if a book is sold, I could very well spend hundreds of hours on a project and come up with zilch!

Step 6: Once an offer comes in or hopefully multiple offers, I help the author decide what comes next. There are different types of offers with territories, terms and advance payments. It's an agent's job to negotiate the terms and, if need be, conduct an auction if multiple houses are interested.

Step 7: Once the contract is signed and sealed an agent will follow up that the advance payment comes in on time, keep track of the writer's schedule for submission if the book is yet to be completed, discuss marketing plans with the author and editor, and serve as a mediator in case of any disputes.

Step 8: Depending on the contract negotiated, the author retains rights for different regions, translation rights or rights such as film, audio etc. which can be sold directly. An agent will reach out to the pertinent people for the same, or—if necessary—engage a sub-agent for the same.

Step 9: Whilst the book is being edited I don't interfere in the process between the editor and author unless there's a difference in opinion, which happens more often than not. Differences can arise on which font works best to the quality of paper to the layout of the book. I need to add though that once a work is sold a publisher can consult an author for all of the above, but they have a right to ultimately do what they feel will be the best fit for the market.

Step 10: Once we have a schedule for print, the author and I contact other authors or prominent personalities for a blurb for the book cover. We also collaborate on book launch ideas, social media marketing, media outreach, book festivals, speaking opportunities etc. For all these tasks the agent receives income based only on commission; the agent is only paid if/when the author is paid.

To sum it up an agent works with the author from the book's conception until the time the book is in stores, and hopefully on a bestseller list. Ultimately I'd like to say that the agent is the author's biggest advocate, and communication between an author and agent is paramount for a good working relationship.

Sherna Khambatta is a literary agent based in Mumbai, India. She holds a Master of Science degree in publishing and is an eclectic reader. She strongly believes that everyone has a story to tell. Her primary focus is non-fiction work. You can get in touch with her via www.shernakhambatta.com.

The Biggest Peeves That Will Put Off An Agent: Mita Kapur

MYSELF, MEERA Sharma, I am a writer who has written her first English-language fictional novel and will be privileged if Sihayi will agree to publish it through your esteemed publication. I have spent last five years working on this fiction very passionaltely. Just last three months I got frustrated and went for self-publishing. It is even more frustrating now so I seek your help in finding a proper publisher. Please find enclosed complete manuscript. I await your reaction in bated breath.

I'm not kidding when I say that this is a standard query letter that we agent's receive. Yup! So, let's lay out the truth folks:

+ Stop introducing yourself as 'myself'.
+ English-language is not hyphenated.
+ Check your cover/query letter for grammar and spelling mistakes.
+ Either call it fiction or a novel; not both.
+ Don't misspell the name of the agency you're submitting to.
+ Don't call an agency a publishing house; do your research.
+ And, if you think that an agency is a publisher, then why are you asking us to find you a "proper publisher"? What does a "proper publisher" even mean?
+ If you've managed to extract the correct email ID from the agency website, then surely you can read the submission

guidelines, which clearly state: "Please send the first three chapters." Why are you then sending us your entire manuscript?

+ We will respond if you follow our submission guidelines, but not if you "keep bating your breath." Which reminds me, we are not interested in your respiratory speed, only your writing.

+ It is only polite and really "proper" if you do not cc other agents and publishers on the same email.

+ It's worse if you send us your submission on a bcc email.

+ It's even worse if your email comes to us as a forwarded email.

+ Since you think the agency is an "esteemed organization", do you also think it's correct to stalk the agent on Facebook?

+ Oh, and if you submit to publishers simultaneously, you're only reducing your chances of us getting you the big bucks.

+ By the way, we love hate mail!

As an agent, I open every submission with anticipation: *Is this the book I'm looking for?* It's been over eleven years but the excitement hasn't waned. But something happens to me when the opening lines of the first chapter are about the sun setting or rising, or the birds chirping, or the river rippling gently. NOOOOOOO. Don't torture me. Then there are sentences when you know the author is thinking in Hindi and writing in English. For God's sake, be honest and write in your mother tongue. The bottom line is that you have to be honest as a writer.

Still, I feel fortunate to add a pulse and rhythm to a book as an agent, and to seeing it out on a bookshelf. It's like seeing your baby flash that toothless smile for the first time. It gives me that rush of maternal pride.

That doesn't mean that it's not frustrating and annoying to deal with publishers who take forever to read and revert, especially when you have to keep reminding your authors to get on with what they're supposed to do best: write. But that's the professional hazard that we opt for as agents. If I were to weigh my annoyances and joys, the joys definitely outweigh the peeves, and I am not saying this to be politically correct. I honestly admit that I groan inwardly when I see some names ringing on my phone—I am not admitting if these are publishers or authors— and I have to grit my teeth in order to be sweet and polite.

Being an agent in India is not a business whopper. It is, in fact, quite the opposite. There are times when the commission is just enough to pay the monthly phone bill. It's too late for us agents now—we are too deep into the commitment to our authors whom we love.

Publishing in India is throwing up new opportunities. It is experimental and challenging. Working with different languages is rewarding and it leads to discovering voices, old and new, which need to reach a wider readership. The roads are open, we need to journey on.

Mita Kapur is the founder and CEO of Siyahi, India's leading literary consultancy. She also conceptualizes and produces literary festivals and events. Her first book, The F-Word, is a food book, memoir, and travelogue. She has edited Chillies and Porridge: Writing Food, an anthology of essays on food. As a freelance journalist, she writes regularly for different newspapers and magazines on social and development issues, along with travel, food, and lifestyle. She is the recipient of Women Super Achiever Award, presented by Femina at the World HRD Congress (2018). She has also received the Maharani Gayatri Devi Award for Woman of Excellence (2014), and the Karamveer Puruskar (2009) for her work as a journalist in creating social awareness, and for being the best literary consultant in the country.

The Journey Of Indian Publishing: Jaya Bhattacharji Rose

AS LONG as I can recall I have wanted to be a publisher. My first 'publication' was a short story in a newspaper when I was a child. Over the years I published book reviews and articles on the publishing industry, such as on the Nai Sarak book market in the heart of old Delhi. These articles were print editions. Back then, owning a computer at home was still a rarity.

In the 1990s, I guest-edited special issues of *The Book Review* on children's and young adult literature at a time when this genre was not even considered a category worth taking note of. Putting together an issue meant using the landline phone preferably during office hours to call publishers/reviewers, or posting letters by snail mail to publishers within India and abroad, hoping some books would arrive in due course. For instance, the first Harry Potter novel came to me via a friend in Chicago who wrote, "Read this. It's a book about a wizard that is selling very well." The next couple of volumes were impossible to get, for at least a few months in India. By the fifth volume, Bloomsbury UK sent me a review copy before the release date, for it was not yet available in India. For the seventh volume a simultaneous release had been organised worldwide. I got my copy the same day from Penguin India, as it was released by Bloomsbury in London (at the time Bloomsbury was still being represented by Penguin India). Publication of this series transformed how the children's literature market was viewed worldwide.

To add variety to these special issues of *The Book Review* I commissioned stories, translations from Indian regional languages (mostly short stories for children), solicited poems, and received lovely ones such as an original poem by Ruskin Bond. All contributions were written in longhand and sent by snail mail, which I would then transfer on to my mother's 486 computer using Word Perfect software. These articles were printed on a Dot matrix printer, backups were made on floppies, and then sent for production. Soon rumours began of a bunch of bright Stanford students who were launching Google. No one was clear what it meant. Meanwhile, the Indian government launched dial-up Internet (mostly unreliable connectivity); nevertheless, we subscribed, although there were few people to send emails to!

The Daryaganj Sunday Bazaar where second-hand books were sold was *the* place to get treasures and international editions. This was unlike today, where there's instant gratification via online retail platforms, such as Amazon and Flipkart, fulfilled usually by local offices of multi-national publishing firms. Before 2000, and the digital boom, most of these did not exist as independent firms in India. Apart from Oxford University Press, some publishers had a presence in India via partnerships: TATA McGraw Hill, HarperCollins with Rupa, and Penguin India with Anand Bazaar Patrika.

From the 1980s, independent presses began to be established like Kali for Women, Tulika and KATHA. 1990s onwards, especially in the noughts, many more appeared— Leftword Books, Three Essays, TARA Books, A&A Trust, Karadi Tales, Navayana, Duckbill Books, Yoda Press, Women Unlimited, Zubaan etc. All this while, publishing houses established by families at the time of Independence or a little before, like Rajpal & Sons, Rajkamal Prakashan,

Vani Prakashan etc continued to do their good work in Hindi publishing. Government organisations like the National Book Trust (NBT) and the Sahitya Akademi were doing sterling work in making literature available from other regional languages, while encouraging children's literature. The NBT organised the bi-annual world book fair (WBF) in Delhi every January. The prominent visibility in the international English language markets of regional language writers, such as Tamil writers Perumal Murugan and Salma (published by Kalachuvadu), so evident today, was a rare phenomenon back then.

In 2000, I wrote the first book market report of India for *Publisher's Association UK*. Since little data existed then, estimating values and size was challenging. So, I created the report based on innumerable conversations with industry veterans and some confidential documents. For years thereafter data from the report was being quoted, as little information on this growing market existed. (Now, of course, with Nielsen Book Scan mapping Indian publishing regularly, we know exact figures, such as: the industry is worth approximately $6 billion.) I was also relatively 'new' to publishing having recently joined feminist publisher Urvashi Butalia's Zubaan. It was an exciting time to be in publishing. Email had arrived. Internet connectivity had sped up processes of communication and production. It was possible to reach out to readers and new markets with regular e-newsletters. Yet, print formats still ruled.

By now multinational publishing houses such as Penguin Random House India, Scholastic India, Pan Macmillan, HarperCollins India, Hachette India, Simon & Schuster India had opened offices in India. These included academic firms like Wiley, Taylor & Francis, Springer, and Pearson too. E-books took a little longer to arrive but they did. Increasingly digital bundles of journal subscriptions began to be sold to institutions by academic publishers, with digital formats favoured over print editions.

Today, easy access to the Internet has exploded the ways of publishing. The Indian publishing industry is thriving

202 The Journey Of Indian Publishing: Jaya Bhattacharji Rose

with self-publishing estimated to be approximately 35% of all business. Genres such as translations, women's writing and children's literature, that were barely considered earlier, are now strong focus areas for publishers. Regional languages are vibrant markets and cross-pollination of translations is actively encouraged. Literary festivals and book launches are thriving. Literary agents have become staple features of the landscape. Book fairs in schools are regular features of school calendars. Titles released worldwide are simultaneously available in India. Online opportunities have made books available in 2 and 3-tier towns of India, which lack physical bookstores. These conveniences are helping bolster readership and fostering a core book market. Now the World Book Fair is held annually and has morphed into a trade fair, frequented by international delegations, with many constructive business transactions happening on the sidelines. In February 2018 the International Publishers Congress was held in India after a gap of 25 years! No wonder India is considered the third largest English language book market of the world! With many regional language markets, India consists of diverse markets within a market. It is set to grow. This hasn't gone unnoticed. In 2017, Livres Canada Books commissioned me to write a report on the Indian book market and the opportunities available for Canadian publishers. This is despite the fact that countries like Canada, whose literature consists mostly of books from France and New York, are typically least interested in other markets.

As an independent publishing consultant I often write on literature and the business of publishing on my blog ... an opportunity that was unthinkable before the Internet boom. At the time of writing the visitor counter on my blog had crossed 5.9 million. The future of publishing is exciting particularly with neural computing transforming the translation landscape and making literature from different cultures rapidly available. Artificial Intelligence (AI) is being experimented with to create short stories. Technological advancements such as print-on-demand are reducing warehousing costs, augmented reality is adding a magical element to traditional forms of storytelling, smartphones with processing chips of 8GB RAM and storage capacities of 256GB seamlessly synchronised with emails and online cloud storage are adding to the heady mix of publishing. Content consumption is happening on electronic devices AND print. E-readers like Kindle are a new form of mechanised process, which are democratizing the publishing process in a manner seen first with Gutenberg and hand presses, and later with the Industrial Revolution and its steam operated printing presses.

The future of publishing is crazily unpredictable and incredibly exciting!

Jaya Bhattacharji Rose is an independent international publishing consultant and columnist who has been associated with the industry for more than twenty-five years. She writes business reports analysing the industry, consulting with publishing firms on business strategies, while also mentoring authors. She has extensive experience including stints with Zubaan, Routledge, and Puffin. Her columns on the business of publishing include "Bibliobibuli" (Times of India online), "PubSpeak" (BusinessWorld online) and "Literati" (The Hindu Literary Supplement). Her articles, interviews, comments and book reviews have appeared in Frontline, The Book Review, DNA, Outlook, The Hoot, The Hindu, Hindustan Times, Brunch, Scroll, Bookwitty.com, LOGOS, BusinessWorld, Housecalls, The Muse, Kitaabnama (Doordarshan), The Guardian, BBC Radio, Radio France and The Independent. Currently she is also a Member, Program Advisory Committee (PAC), for Master of Writing and Publishing, RMIT, Melbourne, Australia.

What You Don't Know About Publishing: Meena Kandasamy

WHEN I was young, I did not personally know a single writer working in English, and I had no clue about publishing: what to do, how to go about it. In a sense, figuring out everything by myself happened to be a blessing in the end because I was rewarded with a lot of experience and life-lessons. I can go on and on, but for the sake of brevity, here are some things I learned the hard way:

1. **Not Every Book Idea Eventually Materializes:** For every single book of yours that gets published and sees the light of day, there will be ten that will sleep in the hard-disks of old dysfunctional laptops, in your parents attic, or on some Internet cloud. Sometimes, you lose work because what you have becomes dated. I worked on a book on decentralisation, the panchayat raj and dalit/women representation, it was meant to be a Black Paper, I got in about 40,000 words, no one other than me ever read it, it never went anywhere. Sometimes you lose work because you have moved on and cannot invest yourself in it anymore. I have at least 10 abandoned non-fiction and translation projects over the last fifteen years. It's okay to feel bad about them, but equally okay to move on and just be happy that any writing experience enriches you.

2. **Invest Your Work In The Small Presses:** Only they have the time, motivation and commitment to invest in you. They will

take wild bets. My first book of translation was published by Stree-Samya in Kolkata, and I approached them over email because they had published Kancha Ilaiah's pathbreaking *Why I Am Not A Hindu*. Mandira Sen agreed to publish my first two books of translation. She's feisty, hard-working and simply brilliant. Other Books in Kerala run by the brilliant Ausaf Ahsan is another example—they roped me, in a very late stage, to work on the biography of Ayyankali—but indirectly this book opened my world, I read so much about Kerala and its history. The same goes for Navayana. I had the chance to meet Anand while I was still in school—and he solidly supported my poetry. I have pitched so many project ideas to him, abandoned many and even absconded with work—but every time it has been a great experience. Yes, the advances might not be great (they may not even exist)—but think of the small press publication as a necessary educational step—like going to school. You will learn things, and you will come out wiser.

3. **Trust Your Instinct In The End:** Editors have years and years of experience, and it is always worthwhile to ask for their input and for their suggestions, but bear in mind that the editor works with the market in mind, and the marketplace is where replicas are far easier to sell. If you are trying out something original, genre-bending, challenging, prepare to be discouraged. Think of that not as a chance to belittle your editor's suggestions, but as a great opportunity to actually stand up for what you believe in, and to passionately defend your own ideas. That will come in very handy when you get annoying audience questions years down the lane.

4. **Let Your Work Be The Best Face You Can Put Forward:** This is not about publishing per se, but about writing. I find a lot of young (and even middle-aged) writers seem to assume that the entire flowchart of writing works in reverse: in their world, one networks with a publisher, gets a book deal, and then retreats to a desk. Chuck the networking, the befriending, the tailing around publishers at literary festivals. Let your work come first. Let your work travel.

5. **Do Not Be Discouraged:** Bad reviews can make you weep—cry your heart out, swear, but get back to the writing desk. Do not judge yourself through shortlists and awards and recognition— publishing is a duckpond, and all of these things are skewed in favour of those who do not ruffle the establishment.

Meena Kandasamy is a Chennai-born London-based poet, novelist and translator. She has published two collections of poetry, Touch (2006) and Ms. Militancy (2010) and has performed her work at literature festivals around the world. She has two novels to her credit, The Gypsy Goddess (2014) and the auto-fictional novel, When I Hit You: Or, the Portrait of the Writer As A Young Wife (2017) which was short-listed for the Women's Prize for Fiction. She was a fellow of the International Writing Program (IWP) at the University of Iowa in 2009, and a British Council Charles Wallace Trust Fellow in 2011. She holds a PhD in sociolinguistics and has written for Al Jazeera, The Hindu, India Today, Himal, Newsweek Middle East, among other places.

Why Good Books Are Rejected:
Kanishka Gupta

SEVERAL YEARS ago, as an aspiring novelist with stardust in my eyes, I would spend most of my waking hours in Yahoo's Books and Literature chatroom, in the company of fellow aspiring writers. I clearly remember how one of the main topics of conversations would be the number of rejection slips one had received on that particular day (or the previous week), agents/ publishers who had requested a partial, and those who had just not bothered to respond. All of us were brought together by the looming sense of uncertainty, suspense, and the palpable realisation that the odds were stacked firmly against us.

Today, having spent more than seven years on the other side, first as a consultant and then as an agent, I think many writers have the wrong notions about rejections. While most books are rejected because of poor quality and incompetence (as they should be), there are several other factors that play a role in publishing decisions:

A Good Book With No Market: Often, good books are rejected at the acquisitions meetings, where people from sales and marketing factor in the target audience, potential print runs, and profit margins. Rejections are relatively more common in case of fiction (especially genre fiction), poetry and short story collections. Several publishers have revised what used to be their minimum print run from 2000/3000 copies to 5000. As a result, books with a dedicated readership and market are being turned down because they are no longer able to justify all the monetary efforts that go into publishing. This somewhat explains the move to publish celebrity or celebrity-driven books, and mass-market books.

A Good Book By A Writer With No Network Or Marketing Abilities: Writers are increasingly being asked to get closely involved with promotional activities for their books. While some of them might be open to the idea, for others it is anathema, as they feel that it is their works that should be doing the talking. One question that is sometimes asked is how many books one will be able to sell within the writer's existing networks, both professional and personal. I pitch some of my proposals with extensive (albeit realistic) marketing plans to improve chances of acceptance. Sometimes one is also asked about the writer's contacts with the media and famous writers/influencers who can be roped in for blurbs and high profile launches. In today's age of literary festivals, it helps to know influential festival directors too! At times, eminently publishable books are rejected in the absence of such contacts or commitments.

A Good Book By A Writer With A Failed Book In The Past: A debut writer is an unknown commodity but for published writers, the receptivity to their new works depends to a great extent on the sales of their previous books. The irony is that this leads to rejection of far superior newer works simply because earlier books didn't have significant sales. In publishing, an unknown debut writer is considered more commercially viable than a known published writer with a bad sales record.

A Good Book In A Genre That A Publisher Has Not Had Success In: Many a time, good books have to pay the price for books in the same genre that failed in the past for a publisher. Some publishers refuse to even consider such books, so quality has very little to do with their decision. Last year, a publishing house rejected an accomplished historical fiction submission despite at least five positive reader reports. Their reasoning: 'Sales feels that a historical fiction in this particular setting hasn't worked for them in the past.' The author ended up putting out a Kindle edition and the book is not available in any bookstores. It took me more than seven months to sell my own editor's high fantasy novel because most publishers felt that Indian fantasy as a genre has just not taken off in the country. Only a handful of editors actually bothered to read what she had written.

Similar Themes: There are only a finite number of ideas that make for compelling full-length books. At times, a book proposal doesn't work because an editor might have published something similar in the past, or is on the verge of doing so. It takes just a few minutes for a savvy commissioning editor to check for already published books on similar themes. I faced this problem while pitching a book on Haldirams by a well-regarded journalist. Just days after our proposal was ready for submission, I learned that a book on this very subject was already ready for printing. This phenomenon is more common in non-fiction (especially biographies and current affairs) than fiction, as in the latter the plot and technique can be significantly different despite a common backdrop.

Evaluation By The Wrong Editor: Often, authors end up sending their submissions to the wrong editor: a commercial novel may end up in a literary editor's inbox and a mind-body-spirit book in the inbox of the current affairs/political editor. At times, the submission might have reached the right editor but he/she may not have an ear for the subject. The more conscientious editor would not like to sign an eminently publishable book if they feel they won't be able to add any value to it. Such misdirected submissions are wasted opportunities, since publishing houses rarely reconsider books, even if they feel an unsuitable editor has read them.

An Editor's Ideology Or Belief System: While this is rare, and one would like to believe that all publishers are objective when it comes to the business of books, a book may be rejected because of an individual editor's prevailing political ideology and personal opinion on a particular subject or personality. Last year, I had a difficult time placing a book on the role of the RSS in the BJP's win in Assam, because quite a few editors didn't want anything to do with a book that endorsed this body. At times, editors reject deserving, eminently marketable biographies/memoirs because they are not admirers of the subjects.

A Good Book That Entails Heavy Production Costs: While we have only a handful of coffee table publishers in the country, books in several other genres, such as graphic novels and high-priced cookbooks, are routinely rejected because of the prohibitive cost of production. The interactive, illustrated nature of such books mean a high production cost, and, thus, lower margins for the publisher.

Kanishka Gupta is South Asia's leading literary agent. He is also a publishing commentator writing for several national and international papers and magazines.

What To Expect In A Publishing Contract: Milee Ashwarya

Q1. What does a standard publishing contract contain?
A standard publishing contract contains the delivery date, the publication date, the royalty, the advance, the title, the genre, ownership, rights, and territory information, to name a few things. It outlines what obligations are expected from the author and the publisher. It covers how sales will be reported. It covers the role of the author in the marketing and publicity of their book.

Q2. What are parts of the contract that are negotiable?
There are a few negotiable bits of the contract like the advance, the delivery date, the rights, the subsidiary rights, and so on.

Q3. What are parts of the contract that are non-negotiable?
Indemnity, legal, termination clauses, etc are non-negotiable. If you're not comfortable with some part of the contract then don't sign on it.

Q4. What should an author do if they can't understand some legal terms and conditions?
Ask the publishers or the contract team for an explanation on any point that's not clear in the contract. There are people who are trained to answer all queries related to publishing contracts. Remember, you're on the same team, so don't treat your publisher like an adversary.

Q5. What are some of the red flags an author should be careful of before signing any contract?

Figure out what you're committing to. These include finances, the rights assigned to publishers, the delivery date, etc. A contract is a legal document and binding by law. Make sure that you read all the clauses carefully before signing the contract.

Q6. Have there been cases of contentious author-publisher fights in India?

Such cases are rare as it is in the interest of both the author and the publisher for the book to be published. However, there have been cases where disputes have arisen between the two parties.

Q7. Can an author break a contract after signing one?

Yes, there are termination clauses both for the author and the publisher.

Q8. Do all publishing houses use the same standard contract or do they differ?

Most of the clauses are standard for all publishing houses. The advance however is specific to each author and book.

Q9. Your advice to authors on negotiating and signing contracts?

Sometimes authors sign a contract without reading it. If you receive an offer that seems fair, you should take it. But don't sign against something without knowing what exactly it asks of you.

Q10. What are some of the most contentious parts of the contract?

The advance and royalties are flashpoints for most authors and publishers. Remember, a low advance does not mean that the publisher does not believe in your work, or that they will not champion your book in the marketplace. Of course, every contract is different and will depend on both the publisher and author. Address any issues you have before signing the contract.

Q11. Does an author ever have to pay the publisher?
No, not unless you're self-publishing.

Q12. How much can an author expect to get paid by the publisher?
Advances in India are typically low, like Rs 10,000 for a new author, and rarely high, a few lakhs for a bestselling author. Royalties are typically 7.5% or more. E-books tend to pay at 15-25% of the MRP.

Q13. Who owns the rights for the book?
An author owns the copyright of their own book, though the publisher registers this for the author. Subsidiary rights crop up in every contract, which means the income a publisher receives from a third party to use the book. This is split with the author. A publisher may ask for tangential rights such as exclusive film/TV rights, eBook/digital rights, audio, hardcover, and paperback rights, all over the world. This means that while the author owns the content of the book, only the publisher is allowed to sell it in the above formats.

Milee Ashwarya is Publisher, Ebury Publishing and Vintage Publishing at Penguin Random House India. Her focus has been on championing the best voices in fiction and non-fiction while publishing a range of bestsellers across segments. Her authors include Prime Minister Narendra Modi, Piyush Pandey, Hussain Zaidi, Yuvraj Singh, Hindol Sengupta, R. Gopalakrishnan, Karan Johar, Ravi Subramanian, Anand Neelakantan, Navi Radjou, Shilpa Shetty, Novoneel Chakraborty, Amjad Ali Khan, Shradha Sharma, Emraan Hashmi, Sonali Bendre, Radhakrishnan Pillai and Payal Gidwani Tiwari to name a few. A TEDx speaker, she is passionate about issues related to working women, parenting and the environment. She was recently awarded the Women Achievers' Samman 2017 for publishing by the Global Organization of People of Indian Origin (GOPIO) and the Distinguished Alumni Award 2017 for Excellence in Publishing by Hindu College, Delhi University.

How To Get Published
Worldwide: Karan Bajaj

Here are the six lessons I've learnt on how to get published that will help you come from nowhere and land a six-figure worldwide book deal:

Your Book Should Crack A Combination Of ENTERTAINMENT And MEANING: A top US literary agent like Mollie Glick, my literary agent, gets 100 queries in one day. Her assistants sieve through them to draw her attention to say, one out of those 100 manuscripts, then she makes one or two representation offers every month. That's a success rate of <0.05%. Then, publishers reject at similar rates. How do you stand out with odds lower than winning a Powerball lottery? Your novel has to jump out of the pages by both entertaining at an epic level and leaving a lingering effect on the reader. If you only entertain, you'll likely be rejected because there are one thousand novelists with existing audiences that are writing about blood sucking vampires and serial killers.

For ENTERTAINMENT, Reveal A "Secret World" Or A Hidden Society In Your Book: Are you revealing a hidden new world about which the reader knows nothing? Think of *The Da Vinci Code's* secret world of holy-grail seekers. Or *Born to Run* with it hidden ultra runners. Or *Harry Potter* and the school of wizards. Your book will jump out among the hundreds of others about dealing with the death of a loved one, or the post-modern angst of living in a big city, or falling in love in college, if you open windows into a new world for your reader instantaneously. You can explore any secret world you are passionate about. I did it with secret yoga ashrams in India. Your story could be set among the Silicon Valley elite, or slumlords playing Russian Roulette in Caracas, anything that gives you a shiver of anticipation just hearing about it and makes you want to research deep into it so that you create an elaborate alternate reality, a fictive dream that your reader can't help but enter.

For MEANING, Give Your Protagonist A Big, Lofty, All-Consuming Goal: At its best, fiction helps you experience a moment of divinity by dissolving your sense of self completely as you're immersed in the new fictive dream. You're experiencing that dream through the story's protagonist so the protagonist's goal should be so big and all-important for them that they—and the reader—are consumed completely by it. Like Ahab chasing Moby Dick. Or Gone Girl's protagonist trying to outdo her husband. Most debut novelists get rejected because their protagonists' goals are either too common or lack urgency.

Use Professional Editors To Edit Your Book Before Submission; The "2,2,2" Rule: You're competing with one hundred manuscripts per day so your book needs to be completely polished before it reaches the desk of a top literary agent. As such, I highly recommend professional editors to lift your writing from debut-quality to expert-quality. This is the "2,2,2" rule that worked for me:

+ Write two full drafts on your own.
+ Then, send it to a developmental editor for strategic comments (story, structure, character trajectory and other fundamental macro issues not copy edits). Cost= $700.
+ Revise two more times based on the development editor's comments.
+ Then, send it to a line editor for a full sentence-by-sentence copy edit. Cost= $2300.

♦   Revise two more times based on the line editor's comments
     and submit your final manuscript to literary agents. With this
     approach, I got a book deal=$95,000 in US, Europe, and India
     (with more foreign rights still being negotiated), an incredible
     ROI on the $3,000 investment in editors.

Create Your Own Hype: This is the exact query letter that got
me a 40% response for a full manuscript from agents, a very
healthy response rate when I compare it to the 10% or so average
I've heard from other writers who've had much more publishing
experience than me.
*Email Subject: Query from #1 Bestselling Indian Novelist: THE
YOGA OF MAX'S DISCONTENT*

Dearest X,
*I was a #1 bestselling novelist in India in 2008 (Keep off the
Grass, HarperCollins India) and 2010 (Johnny Gone down,
HarperCollins India) with 150,000+ copies of my novels in print.
Both novels have been optioned into films, currently in different
stages of development. I seek representation for my 3rd novel, THE
YOGA OF MAX'S DISCONTENT (70,000 words, mainstream
fiction), my first novel targeted for a US audience.*

*About the novel: A violent encounter forces Maximus Pzoras, a
Harvard economist and Wall Street banker, to confront questions
about suffering and mortality that have dogged him since his mother's
death. His search for a mentor takes him from Manhattan to the
dark underbelly of India to a near-fatal hike up the Himalayas and
finally, a small drought stricken village in South India where strange
things begin to happen to him: he remembers past lives, he can
levitate and walk on water, do impossible Yoga poses and glimpse
future events. Max struggles to overcome his rational skepticism
and the love of his family pulling him back home. In a final bid for
answers, he embarks on dangerous solitary meditation in a freezing
Himalayan cave. Will Max, Wall Street banker turned Himalayan*

sage, penetrate the truth of human suffering? Is enlightenment just a new age illusion or an accessible truth?

The YOGA OF MAX'S DISCONTENT is a pulsating, contemporary take on the classic human quest for transcendence, a Siddhartha for our generation. I could think of no better agent to represent my US debut given your stated passion for culture-defining books that make a difference in the world-exactly what I strove for in my story, which is both a page-turning journey through India and a journey of tremendous inner transformation. I would be deeply obliged if you could consider my query.

Thank you,
Karan

Note the first paragraph. I didn't say, "I'm a published author in India." I gave very specific, compelling statistics that made my query and subject line pop. You may argue that mine was a unique case but look closely at your own background—you'll find specific, tangible achievements you can use. For example, if you had one short story published in the New Delhi Literary journal, don't do what 99% of authors do and say: "I'm a published writer with several short stories." Instead, try this harder hitting copy option: "My most recent short story, published in the New Delhi Literary Journal, was voted as the #1 short story in a reader survey and was reviewed as "X's voice explodes with narrative force" by a prominent critic."

Immediately, perception shifts. And to enable a claim like this, all you need to do is to conduct your own reader survey testing story descriptions from other stories in the New Delhi literary journal on Survey Monkey for free. Be inventive. Create your own hype. No one else will do it for you as a debut novelist.

Build Scarcity Into Your Pitch: This is the follow-up letter I'd send to every agent within ten days of sending my original query.

Email Subject: FW: Query from #1 Bestselling Indian Novelist:
THE YOGA OF MAX'S DISCONTENT

Dearest X,

No intention to hurry you whatsoever as I know it takes more time
to evaluate a query and I fully respect your process.

I just wanted to keep you in the loop that two of the agents I sent my first
set of queries to responded with a request for a full, somewhat surprisingly
for my understanding of the longer timelines in the US publishing process.

Since you were at the top of my desired list because of your confluence
of interests in commercial fiction and religion/ spirituality, I was
really eager for your response. If at all your time allows, I would be
very grateful if you could tell me of your interest.

Thank you,
Karan

I'd send this letter out to every agent the moment I heard a vaguely
positive response from another agent. Note, the feeling of scarcity
in this pitch. Almost always, the agent I sent it to would review
the manuscript immediately, an exception in an industry where it
can take upto three months for an agent to review a manuscript.
After I received an agent offer, I'd be even more straightforward
in my outreach to other agents.

Dearest X,

I wanted to let you know that things moved rather quickly and I
have received an agent representation offer. I have requested a week
ending Monday, Aug 26, to make my decision.

As I stated in my very heartfelt query below, I'm very interested in hearing from you so if your time/interest permits, it would be great for me to know your interest in reviewing the manuscript this week.

Thank you,
Karan

Without this urgency, the agent has no motivation to give you a priority over the hundreds of queries in the slush-pile. Use similar scarcity triggers anywhere you can in the process to speed up a notoriously slow industry.

Use the above approach, first to write a great novel, then to get a top US literary agent because a top agent is the difference between your manuscript languishing for months with an intern at a publishing house vs. being sent to the senior commissioning editor who has the discretion to make an immediate offer (Mollie Glick, my agent, got me multiple offers within nine days of submitting my manuscript for perspective). And you're on your way to get a worldwide book deal!

Karan Bajaj is an Indian American author of three contemporary Indian novels, Keep Off the Grass, Johnny Gone Down and The Seeker.

How To Publish Abroad:
Michael Dwyer

My introduction to publishing in India occurred long before I first went there, in the form of the neatly composed, hand-written letters that were delivered to our office in Covent Garden. On opening the heavily stamped manila envelopes I realised that my then boss, Christopher Hurst, had met his match. His correspondent was P.K. Ghosh, a printer and publisher from Calcutta, Bengal's literary heartland. They were engaged in a titanic struggle, one of competitive fastidiousness, which lasted for years.

Christopher was a hot-metal head, fascinated by the casting of type, leading and alignment, widows and orphans. So was Mr Ghosh. Thus began a long-distance bromance as they painstakingly debated the aesthetic and practical merits of one running head or another, all while working together on the typesetting of what was to be K.M. De Silva's *A History of Sri Lanka*.

The Permit Raj frowned on innovation, which suited our Bengali typesetter. It also fostered a culture of make do and mend. That sensibility, almost an objective in itself, when dovetailed with the absurdly well-read men and women who dominated Indian publishing before liberalisation in 1991, meant that the book scene was resolutely organic, quietly self-possessed and modest to a fault. Its exemplars were Popular Prakashan and Orient Longman, two regional houses that celebrated their allegedly peripheral status by publishing classics by local authors in regional languages, as well as English. Its luminaries of one generation included Neil O'Brien, Ravi Dayal, J. Rameshwar Rao; and of another Rukun Advani, Urvashi Butalia, David Davidar, Pramod Kapoor and Ravi Singh.

As I never read books, I will resist the temptation of digressing about the writers India was producing at this time. Their evident merits and achievements are now a global commonplace. They produced a formidable literary canon that opens India's soft power batting order.

Exchange controls were such that selling rights into India was tough, so literary traffic flowed in the other direction, with our firm acquiring rights and republishing in Britain and America for books from India. At that time, and still today, indigenous publishing in Pakistan, Bangladesh and Nepal remained a mystery, in contrast to the vibrancy manifested in India.

Before the advent of the computer, mobile phone and laptop, one cracked and dusty Old Delhi street was Indian publishing's Silicon Valley, where ideas came from and deals were done. I remember failing to get to Daryaganj on several occasions. Once my rickshaw driver took me elsewhere, up towards the Ridge; another time I got close, then turned back, having surrendered to the heat; and on a third expedition I reached my objective, my personal Tiger Hill, but ran away, ashamed, after failing to find even one of the three offices I had come to visit. It was like that, then. A myth of my own making, the journey not the arrival, a street of books and bookmen known to everyone but me.

Now one speeds along NH-this-and-that to freshly painted concrete towers. This is where one finds Indian publishers. Their natural habitat has changed, and so have their habits. Khadi waistcoats are rarer than they were, some drive Innovas and Qualis, many hang out in cocktail bars, they all do Jaipur, holiday in Goa or Nainital.

The editors shift from tower to tower every few years, reconnecting with old friends, former colleagues and, of course, authors they've worked with. Email confusion results. My poor inbox sees the same names reappearing again and again, year after year, though with different suffixes, often that of a foreign publishing behemoth, now comfortably bedded down in the new Klondike of English and, increasingly, indigenous language publishing.

They publish more foreign books than hitherto. Other publishers eagerly plunder their lists, as do I, seeking fine writing, fabulous stories, dazzling fiction and non-fiction. The hunt never ends, the books keep coming: think Snigdha Poonam's *Dreamers* or Shashi Tharoor's *Why I Am A Hindu*. The ones that didn't get away, the ones that make people smile with appreciation.

So, how do overseas publishers acquire books from India? By networking in India, meeting Indian publishers at the Frankfurt, London and Delhi book fairs, and attending literary festivals, where editors often have far more time on their hands than when behind a desk. They also look out for leading book reviews via print and online locations—the Indian press, sites such as The Wire and Scroll, the Indian Review of Books. They interact with agents in India and elsewhere who specialise in writing from the subcontinent. Above all, they get on the road and meet colleagues and fellow editors from among the great range of Indian publishing houses.

As for Indian authors looking to place their books with a foreign publisher, an agent is a must-have, either in India or overseas, if you're writing fiction. Non-fiction authors can scour publishers' websites to find those whose list matches their own interests, and approach them directly, whether in Britain, America or elsewhere. Alternatively, why not publish your book first with an Indian publisher and let them sell the rights to a foreign house, or—better still—retain those (non-Indian) rights yourself? Book markets are increasingly interlinked in the age of

Amazon, so geography ought not to hinder one's quest to get published worldwide. It's much easier than it used to be, even though your letters won't be set in hot metal by P.K. Ghosh.

Michael Dwyer is the Publisher & MD of C. Hurst & Co. (Publishers) Ltd., an independent non-fiction publisher based in London.

What Works In Regional Language Publishing: Neeta Gupta

SOCIAL MEDIA has completely transformed the publishing landscape in Indian languages, especially for millennials. While in the 'olden days', publishers depended on senior writers and critics, or even friends, to recommend new voices, Facebook, Twitter and Instagram have changed all that. Bold, new writing is emerging in Bangla, Telugu, Kannada, Hindi, Tamil among many others.

Traditionally, in Marathi, for instance, Diwali Visheshanks or special Diwali issues of literary magazines featured new writing and new voices that would go on to make a name for themselves. The celebrated Kannada writer Vivek Shanbhag says, "Popular [Kannada] newspapers have annual story competitions which is one of the ways of discovering new talent. There are some awards for the unpublished works which come in the form of support for the publication of the work. A publication called Chandha Pusthaka has an award for an unpublished first book. The winner not only gets the award money but also gets the opportunity to get the book published by Chandha Pusthaka. Of course, [the] grapevine is still the most powerful of all [routes to discovering new talent]."

These were the traditional sources for publishers to seek out new talent. But these spaces had gatekeepers: editors who had the power to accept or reject a submission. The digital space has changed that. What started out as popular blog writing in the early 2000s has now been taken over by social media influencers in different languages, a phenomenon that publishers are increasingly taking note of. This can be seen by the tremendous success of the LaPreK (Laghu Prem Katha) series published by Rajkamal Prakashan, in which a collection of Facebook posts by the iconic journalist Ravish Kumar became an overnight publishing sensation. Esha Chatterjee (Bee Books) says, "A lot of new voices are writing in Bengali and the popularity is visible through likes and comments [on Facebook]. The subjects that the writers are choosing are unique and more daring than what popularly existed earlier. These authors have a set of readers already, which ensures a certain commercial success for the books."

Publishers like Shailesh Bharatwasi (Hind Yugm) have brazenly leveraged this trend by publishing very contemporary writing in Hindi and introduced the concept of 'pre-order' for Hindi books on Amazon and Flipkart, thereby gauging their own print run in advance by announcing these pre-orders on Facebook, for instance. Bharatwasi admits that if there was no social media, "our business will be reduced by 90%".

Aditi Maheshwari Goyal, a third-generation publisher at Vani Prakashan, claims that she receives about 4-5 manuscripts a day, and sometimes over 200 manuscripts a month! Chatterjee receives about 30-35 Bengali manuscripts a month. Most of these are handwritten. Clearly, it is not possible for either of them to publish all these books and as a result new authors constitute only about 10-15% of their annual list.

Satyanand Singh Nirupam (Chief Editor, Rajkamal Prakashan) bemoans the lack of an editorial structure in the Hindi publishing industry. While in the Western publishing model (and even in the English language publishing houses in India), the editor plays a key role—she or he works closely with the author and with the marketing, sales, design and other departments to deliver a successful book—this is unfortunately not the case in Indian language publishing. Most publishing houses have only proof readers and traditionally an author has to double up as his or her own editor.

Nirupam also says that keeping in mind the needs of contemporary readers, he keeps a close watch on what's being written in the media and very often picks and chooses a new writer based on their writing in print and digital spaces. He might commission a book based on a writer's style, asking them to develop an idea that may already have some traction. In such cases, he prefers to work with new writers, unless the idea is so subject-specific that it needs an expert from that particular field.

Translations into Indian languages are increasingly becoming popular, especially when it comes to non-fiction, self-help, lifestyle and aspirational books. The success of translations into Indian languages can be gauged by the fact that the Dainik Jagran/Nielsen bestseller listings have a separate category for translations into Hindi. Popular authors like Amish Tripathi of Westland/Amazon have successfully been translated into every major Indian language with competitive sales figures running into lakhs of copies. Traditionally, a book is declared a bestseller in an Indian language if it sells over 5000 copies.

In terms of contracts and copyrights, Indian language publishers used to have a pretty lax attitude as far as paperwork was concerned. Book deals were made over a handshake and very often an author would be happy to get a gift hamper on Diwali to celebrate a successful book. But the trend has changed in this generation. As Aditi concurs, "I am glad that new authors understand the importance of MOUs (Memorandum of Understanding) and copyright agreements, and honour them."

Increasingly, content created in the languages is in great demand for contemporary web series, YouTube content, or film and digital media. As a result, publishers in Indian languages have to also take on the agent's role for their authors, and coordinate with production houses and digital media to meet their unending need for locally relevant content. Bharatwasi confirms, "We are continuously in the process of seeking digital convergences. We have already contracted with Audible to prepare an audio version of almost all the books published till 2017. We are consistently in negotiations with Amazon Prime Video and Netflix Digital whenever we bring out a new book. The sale of film rights for two books is in fact in the final phase. We have been in touch with many production companies. I believe that books in Indian languages are more likely to succeed in the new media. This trend has also given a new lease of life to publishers' backlists of long-form literature and classical narratives in the languages."

Indian publishers also represent their authors for translation into other languages, both Indian and international. Kannan Sundaram (Kalachuvadu), for instance, travels regularly to Frankfurt and other rights fairs to showcase and sell foreign language rights for his authors' works.

In the last 5-10 years, one has seen a spurt in the number of Indian language translations into English as well. While I hesitate to define anything as a trend, more and more Indian writing is being published in English translation, both in India and abroad. Many of the readers for these translations tend to be Indians, as well as South Asian diasporic readers, for whom reading these translations is like returning to their roots.

Indian language publishing gets massive support from state library purchases. This is a double-edged sword. While on one hand, it encourages publishers to take on 'good' literary works which they may not otherwise find commercially viable, on the other hand, it tends to make publishers lazy in terms of sales and distribution because central library purchases guarantee a certain minimum order. Social media comes to the rescue again by providing a free space for posting book reviews and endorsements. In times when print media space for book reviews are shrinking, language publishers are resorting to Twitter and Facebook to stay in touch with their readers.

They are also learning to use algorithms to maximize discoverability on online platforms.

Audio books and e-books have also made a huge impact in the languages. In a country with a billion mobile phone users, audio book companies like StoryTel and Audible are launching in a big way. Just a few years ago Dailyhunt had launched a regional language news and e-books application which was used by over 95 million users, 95% of whom consumed the content in their own language. With over 100,000 books and 600 Publishers in 15 Indian languages, it had one of the largest networks for e-books in India. There are of course many more players in this field today.

In the end, we may need some reflection on what these trends imply. In what way is the democratisation of literature in the age of social media leading to an irreversible decline in the way we think about, create and consume literature—no matter what the genre? As publishers are we only accepting works that are trending? Is saleability the only criterion?

Neeta Gupta is the publisher at Yatra Books, and an editor and Joint Secretary with the Bhartiya Anuvad Parishad, a not-for-profit promoting translations between Indian languages. She is also the Festival co-director for Jaipur BookMark, a publishers' B2B segment held parallel to the ZEE Jaipur Literature Festival, where the focus is translation.

How Book Distribution In India Works: Santosh Pandey

I HAVE been in the book trade business for almost 38 years. Over the last three decades I have seen many ups and downs. At one time distributors used to import books directly from abroad, especially from all the big UK and USA publishers. Now most of these foreign publishers have opened up offices in India, for trading in terms of holding stocks, and for publishing in India. Due to this trend, distributors are facing a tough time. Even after trading with retail channels, to ensure that titles reach every retailer, we are facing the issue of narrow margins.

On the other hand, a lot of Indian authors have been successful and build a big name for themselves, as they are writing for and publishing with these big publishing houses. We are seeing that the sales numbers of Indian authors are in par with foreign authors. It is therefore good for new authors to leverage these publishing houses in order to bring their work and talent to the forefront and gain both Indian and foreign readers.

Indian publishing is booming and it is expected to reach greater heights in the times to come. Another factor that is contributing to this growth is the entry of online stores like Amazon and many Indian sellers over the past few years. Thanks to the option of online promos we find that awareness about authors and publishers is reaching new heights.

The biggest concern in the book industry currently is that offline stores are facing a tough time. The online book distribution system has affected them to a certain extent. It is well-known that this is now just a question of survival. Offline stores are developing their own strategy in order to survive, at least in the near future, such that they overcome the current down fall. Despite these changes and concerns, we are seeing that the overall book trade is growing and we hope that it grows even more in the coming times.

Many new authors are uncertain about how the book distribution system works. Distribution is simply the process by which a book is made available to a reader. The system is also fairly straightforward. The publisher sends books from their printing press to distributors and wholesalers like us at IBD (India Book Distributors Ltd.). Most distributors are big stockists who look after a particular region, like West India or North India, or a particular state, like Maharashtra or Karnataka. From the distributor, the book goes to the retailer. The retailer can be your small mom-and-pop shop or a big bookstore chain like Crossword. From this retailer a reader purchases books.

The margins for distributors left after trading are very minimal. After distribution of titles in retail trade, we get only 5-10% of the selling price of the book. So, if a book is priced at Rs 100, we will get around Rs 5-10, while a retailer—offline or online—will get Rs 40-60, which is a discount of around 40-60%. To protect ourselves, we work on the term that if a book does not sell within a specific time frame, like three or six months, the book is fully returnable.

If you are self-publishing a book it can be tough to get a distributor. Due to our overheads of storing book copies and our costs in selling books to retailers, we have to be careful about the books that we do decide to distribute. We normally select books that have a higher probability of being picked up by retailers and readers. We also don't make an upfront payment in order to negate financial risk.

Sometimes we face criticism about the book of a particular author or a particular title not being available or being out of stock at a bookstore. This is because in certain cities, like Mumbai, space constraints are a big issue. Due to the number of new titles that are published every month, which have a huge range in terms of categories like fiction, non-fiction and children's books, it becomes difficult to keep track of and visibility on each and every book title or author.

If an author wants to ensure that their book is in each store, one way is to create awareness among readers with the help of promotions and print media support. When a bookseller sees the demand for a book arising, they will not want to lose out on sales and will therefore keep a good quantity of that book title on their shelves. Another influencing factor is pre-booking numbers on big online stores that take place before the release of an author's title. This plays a vital role for trade and for readers.

All said and done, we are sure that we are heading for a golden time for both authors and publishers in India.

Santosh Pandey is a manager at MMC Mumbai, a unit of India Book Distributors (Bombay) Ltd.

How To Design A Good Book Cover: Pinaki De

ONE OF the primary and literal aims of the cover designer is to capture eyeballs, to direct the gaze of the spectator towards a particular book among a mélange in a bookstore. Once the book is picked from the crowd of books the primary job of the designer is done.

Naturally it takes a certain kind of intellectual expertise to make a truly great cover. In many covers, there's a deliberate attempt to create artificial symbolism for instant impact. It works like a clever advertising one-liner. Sadly, in these cases, nothing can move deeper or beyond. Of course, in the market place, everything works until you blink. However, one of the challenges of a cover designer is not simply to pluck an isolated image from the text itself but to dwell on textual details that can support the metaphoric weight of the entire book. The book should literally or tangentially reflect the trajectory of its content rather than just positing a good-looking image.

Master designer Peter Mendelsund's wonderfully minimalist cover designs show how he has transformed those books into testaments of perception, identity and vision. In this manner, the book cover captures the essence of the book in some fundamental and perhaps unforeseen way. That, of course, entails a reading a manuscript closely enough. In other words, making a great book cover isn't just about 'making'. It starts with reading and understanding. Once the designer has internalized a manuscript, he/she can draw his/her preliminary ideas on paper/tablet. It is always better to make as many doodles as possible before one decides to nurture two to three good options. At this stage, one can talk with the editor in order to integrate the initial ideas with the cover brief. It's important to be experimental here otherwise one can get stuck within a given vision.

The primary job of the designer is to extend the vision of the cover brief, not to be limited by it. This is where the creative instinct of the designer comes to play. The ideation is the most crucial element of a cover design. Then the idea needs to be executed. The execution depends on the skillset that an individual designer has developed. Depending on the need of a particular cover, one can use photographs (either specially commissioned for the book or stock photographs from various sources), paintings, illustrations, mixed media work, collages, handwritten script and so on. There is no sure-shot formula for a great cover. Sometimes a simple typography works better than all the above. As a designer it is extremely important to be an expert on typography. It is a sensitive subject and requires a lot of erudite reading. Random use of any typeface that a designer takes a liking to is not at all desired. The type should complement the work done on the cover.

Another crucial aspect of book cover design is the judicious use of negative space or white space. In art, negative or white space refers to the space around and between the subject(s) of an image. In graphic design of printed materials (like a book cover), where effective communication is the objective, the use of negative space may be crucial. I feel Indian book covers have too many design elements and are way too cluttered to make an immediate impact in a bookshop. A minimalist treatment with ample negative space often enhances the chance of drawing the reader's attention. For an artist, it is imperative to understand the dynamics of the negative space that he/she needs to leave blank more than the positive space that he/she wants to fill up with his/her own handiwork. The balance that an artist achieves here will decide the aesthetic quality of the work.

The covers that we see in the public domain are eternally haunted by the ones that never made it—those that exist as specters in the cold storage of the artist's memory or in their computer/studios. They are vestiges of a painful rejection process that every designer goes through. Sometimes the reasons for rejections are valid and sometimes they are downright ridiculous, as they do not conform to a certain pattern. For a certain contingent of the publishing industry, book designing means playing it safe. The path of least resistance is to design a jacket and give that particular demographic exactly what they want. It is only when the untrodden path is taken, a truly beautiful work of art emerges. Otherwise we are left with a blank page that stares back at our own emptiness.

A frequent question that crops up in many discussions is about the process of locating a good designer by a newbie author. If the author manages to get a good publisher, then the job is almost done. Big publishing houses have their own art director who can easily assign the said cover to a competent in-house designer or a proven freelance designer. In India, most of the publishing houses have their own roster of freelance designers to choose from. Sometimes, the author can recommend a designer whom he/she prefers, but the final decision of assigning a work rests on the collective wisdom of the publishing house. That said, although the bulk of my own work comes through publishers, sometimes I do take up freelance assignments directly from authors, although these are few in number. If you're looking to find a good book designer, it's a task in India. Unfortunately, we don't have reliable sites like say www.99designs.com. The ones we have don't list quality designers at all. Therefore, Facebook works best in India in case of finding freelance designers.

If you're looking to become a book designer then a design degree from a reputed institute may help in getting a job as an art director of a publishing house, but it is in no way a guarantee of getting quality work. Ultimately the work speaks more than anything else. I have no formal art degree. In fact, I have a day job as an Associate Professor of English in a college under University of Calcutta. However, as a student of English literature in Jadavpur University, I started doing mock covers of books as a hobby and graduated to designing covers of academic books penned by my teachers. My big break came in 2000 when my teacher, Nilanjana Gupta, assigned me to design the cover of a book she had written for Penguin India. The design team of Penguin liked the cover and gave me work. Once I got noticed in the publishing scene, things began to fall into place. I was then picked up by Harper Collins India and subsequently worked with almost all the top-line publishers of the country. For a new designer with no prior experience, it can be rewarding to redo covers of books that you don't like. The mock covers can be put together in a hardbound/digital portfolio, which can be handy in getting your first assignment.

Remember, cover designers are not given their due in the publishing industry. The payment is still low, as compared to the global standard, and many freelancers in India do this work for passion, more than the money involved. Things are much better if one gets a job as a full-time designer in a publishing house, although such posts are few.

There is nothing like a trend in the world of designing. Most times it's better to set a trend rather than blindly follow things in vogue. Often, it's a welcome diversion for a designer to go to a bookshop and see what others are doing with books of various genres. Alternatively, one can also search specialized websites like www.bookcoverarchive.com or Pinterest boards of book covers. This way a designer can stay updated with new work across the globe.

Pinaki De is an Associate Professor of English Literature in a college affiliated to the University of Calcutta. He is also a well-known graphic designer and illustrator who has done numerous book covers for publishers like Penguin Random House, Harper Collins, Hachette, OUP, Simon and Schuster, Pan Macmillan, Bloomsbury, Rupa, Amaryllis, Primus Books, Singapore University Press (NUS), Orient Blackswan, Routledge and others. Recently he won the coveted Oxford Bookstore Cover Prize 2017 at Jaipur Literature Festival. He also won the 2017 Publishing Next award for the best cover. A Charles Wallace Trust Fellow, he is the Indian Comics Advisor to the global exhibition titled "Mangasia: Wonderlands of Indian Comics" curated by the legendary Paul Gravett and organised by The Barbican, London.

Self-Publish The Right Way: Anup Jerajani

TONI MORRISON, the acclaimed American novelist, once said, '*If there's a book that you want to read, but it hasn't been written yet, then you must write it.*' I completely agree with this.

We are all storytellers. We all have ideas that we want to share with the world. What's better than penning our thoughts into a book, to be read by present and future generations?

As a book buyer for Crossword Bookstores, I used to come across people expressing their desire to be writers or to sell their books well. Some came with published books, which they wished to sell from our stores. Others expressed a desire to get their books published with a traditional publisher. Some needed guidance on how to start writing a book.

As booksellers all we could do was guide these people to approach the publishers we knew. However, most of these unpublished authors would end up disappointed since none of the mainstream publishers showed interest in their work. This was even though some of the raw manuscripts we came across were genuinely well-written.

A few years ago with the digital and e-commerce advent, a lot of online self-publishing companies took birth. These same set of authors started getting in touch with these companies to get their books published. However, self-publishing online came with limitations. There was no guarantee that the book published by these companies would go through a proper pre-press process (edit, design, typeset etc.), which is crucial for a well-published book. Many authors would end up with poor quality books, both in terms of content and printing. Since these books were print-on-demand they were only available online. Most of the books would hardly sell as they'd get lost in the plethora of books listed on online sites.

The same set of authors would approach us again wanting their books to be placed in Crossword stores. However, like any industry, we have our own ecosystem and distribution channel in the book trade, making it impossible to start dealing with authors directly. Authors do not understand this and become dejected when they don't see their books in bookstores.

Seeing these trends we realised an opportunity to help authors get their books published professionally in terms of prepress, production, and distribution across our 90 stores and in major online bookstores. After much research and study, in 2014 we launched our in-house publishing platform: The Write Place Publishing. This publishing initiative by Crossword Bookstores Ltd. began with the aim to enable aspiring authors convert their stories into a finished book, and to connect them to the right audience. So far, we've published 70-plus books in different genres and have more than 33 books in different stages of publishing.

If you're looking to self-publish, then here are some tips:

Decide When To Self-Publish: Self-publishing is not only for authors who are rejected by traditional publishers. There are many reasons that authors choose to self-publish. Some authors want books available to a niche audience, like their community. Some want their books to come out quickly, which traditional publishing does not offer. Some like the transparency of the process. Some like the fact that there is revenue-sharing model versus a royalty's model, which can leave the author with more money if the book crosses a certain sale number.

Some published authors also self-publish, as they want to publish their book on their own and have control over the rights and process. While it is widely believed that every author wants to publish traditionally, this is not true at all.

Find The Right Self-Publishing Platform: Look out for self-publishing companies with a good publishing record. Have a look at their past catalog. See their track record to see the quality of their work. Check the editing and print quality of their published books. It's important to know their distribution network in physical stores. Honestly, a new author is only discovered in a physical store.

Send A Good Query Letter: Publishers get scores of queries and manuscripts on a daily basis. It's important that the query sent by an author is short, crisp and yet covers everything. You should send at least 4 chapters of the manuscript, a table of contents, a short synopsis of the book, the number of words of the complete manuscript, and—most important of all—a short bio. The publisher wants to know who the author is.

Send Good Sample Chapters: If the publisher finds the initial query and chapters interesting, they may ask for the complete manuscript or more sample chapters. Send your best ones.

Meet: If the author and publisher are based in the same city, and if it is possible to meet, I would suggest a brief meeting with the publisher/editor, as it is sometimes easier to express your thoughts in person. Do this only if the publisher/editor is interested. Don't badger them if they're not. You'll be blacklisted.

Find An Editor, Designer And Printer: It's always better to let the publisher take care of all things pertaining to the publishing of the book. All good publishers have a decent pool of editors, designers, as well as printers.

Publish Your Book Well: Spell check. Make sure that your book has no grammatical mistakes. Make sure the typeset is done. Make sure the book is properly converted to an eBook format. Make sure you own the copyright as with traditional publishing (the ISBN is something that the publisher applies for). Go to specialists, as many online self-publishing platforms are not good at providing these services. A self-published book should look as professional as a traditionally published book.

Market Your Book Well: Every author wants to be the next Amish or Chetan Bhagat. Your book will not sell like an FMCG product. You will not be called to all the lit fests. Remove such assumptions. Be proactive in selling your book. A publisher's job is to print and distribute your book. It is your job to sell and promote your book. Build your brand patiently over years. Be aware that book selling is a lengthy and tedious process.

What Makes A Bestseller: There are no exact industry figures or definite quantity to what makes a book a bestseller. It also depends on the genre. If you're writing commercial fiction then make sure you sell 10,000 copies within one year. If you're writing literary fiction then make sure you sell 5,000 copies within one year. It also depends on the author. If only 50,000 copies of a Chetan Bhagat book sell, then it may not be considered a bestseller. But if a literary fiction book sells so much it will be considered a mega-bestseller. A bestseller also depends on the time. Some books don't sell for 15-16 years, like Moby-Dick, which sold 500 copies initially and now sells in millions. A self-published book should sell 2000-3000 copies to be considered a bestselling book and for the author to recover the money they've invested.

How Do Payments Work: Payments in self-publishing work somewhat like they do in traditional publishing. Traditional distributors get a 50-60% discount from publishers, and give a 35-40% discount to booksellers. The publisher gets 40% in profits, but has to account for costs incurred in publishing that book. Since an author is also the publisher in self-publishing, expect to get 40-45% in royalties on MRP, or between 50-60% in royalties on net receipts. Don't expect an advance, as the author needs to pay to get the book self-published. The royalty payment is scheduled every month or quarter depending on the publisher, versus traditional publishing where the cycle is bi-annual or annual due to the four-month credit cycle in book selling. If your self-published book sells well, you will get to make more money than in traditional publishing.

What Not To Do In Self-Publishing: Don't delve too much into perfecting the manuscript before it's given to the publisher. Once the book is written and you have decided to go ahead with the publishing process, don't show your work to many different people. Showing your unpublished book to husbands, in-laws, cousins, friends and colleagues at the same time will leave you overwhelmed because everyone will have a different opinion and will end up suggesting changes. In this case, too many cooks will spoil the broth, and you'll end up confused. Trust only one or two people. Trust your editor. Don't make your editor miserable. Have a clear viewpoint on your book. Ultimately, listen to everyone, but do what you want. Don't expect your book to be at every airport, railway station or bookstore as retail stores have very specific spaces allotted to very specific books. Good luck!

Anup Jerajani is a third-generation bookseller who has been with Crossword Bookstores Ltd. for the last 13 years. As a part of the books buying and merchandising team, and as the Head of Publishing and Lifestyle Categories, he has vast experience in book selling and publishing. Anup conceptualized and spearheaded 'The Write Place Publishing', Crossword's in-house publishing program.

How To Go From Self-Published
Author To Bestselling Author:
Ashwin Sanghi

MANY YEARS ago at a literary event, a member of the audience asked me, 'What are the factors that contributed to your success as an author?' My reply was probably unlike anything that she expected.

I recounted an anecdote from my own writing journey. Having completed my first novel, I was in the process of making submissions to literary agents and publishers. After sending out a little over a hundred letters, I was sorely disappointed when polite and not-so-polite rejections arrived. In fact, the vast majority did not reply at all. A year later, it was evident to me that no one was really interested in my work.

I described my situation to a close family friend who was having dinner with my father. Taking a generous gulp of his third peg of Johnnie Walker Black Label, the gregarious Punjabi gentleman responded, 'In life, ninety-nine per cent is about good luck! Just remember that, son.'

I was in an argumentative mood and I pressed the point. 'But uncle, what about the balance one per cent? Surely that must be related to hard work, talent, efficiency, network or resources?'

Laughing loudly, my father's friend declared triumphantly, 'The final one per cent? That's called bloody good luck, my boy! Simply keep at it and wait for your bloody good luck to kick in!'

Today, I realize that the key operative terms in his statement were 'keep at it' and 'wait'. There are possibly thousands of exceptional manuscripts that never became bestsellers. Why? Simply because their authors did not have the patience or persistence to market them.

After being rejected by most literary agents and publishers, I realized that my attempts to get published the traditional way in India had come to naught, and that I was at a dead end. I took the decision to self-publish my first novel via a US-based self-publishing platform that specialized in Print-On-Demand or POD (remember that these were pre-Kindle times). One simply uploaded a PDF file of one's book to the company's server, designed a simple cover and acquired an ISBN. The book would then get listed on major retail websites and an order would trigger a single print of the book that would be door-delivered to the customer.

I soon realized that the platform was selling my books only via American online retail channels and my title remained unavailable in Indian bookstores. Even with my best efforts on social media I was unable to sell more than a couple of books each day. To add to my woes, a key reviewer suggested that my book could have been shorter. In her view, the book should have stopped on page ten! Ouch! I was disheartened but I plodded on.

I began making the rounds of bookstores in India to find out if they would be willing to keep a few of my books on consignment basis—they would only have to pay me if copies were actually sold. None of them were willing to do that. They bought their stock from distributors, not individual authors. 'Find a distributor,' was the standard refrain.

By this time I had given up any hope of getting published the traditional way. All that I wanted now was to find an appropriate distributor in India. One of my friends had worked for eighteen years with a very large textbook distribution outfit in India. He shared with me a list of some key Indian distributors. He advised me to write to each of them individually, enclosing a copy of my book. After sending out a hundred books, I waited. And waited. And then some more.

After several months of no replies, I finally received a call. It was from a lady who was one among the hundred distributors I had reached out to. I did not know it at that time, but she was the founder of chain of bookstores and her company had just created a publishing joint venture. She told me that she loved my novel but it would be impossible to import the book from America and then expect to sell it in the Indian market at a reasonable price. Would I be willing to republish it in India? I jumped with joy at her question. I had been turned down by almost every publisher on the planet by then. We signed a contract two weeks later—almost four years after I'd completed the manuscript.

One of the conditions of the contract was that I would be willing to undertake rewrites and edits. I did not give it much thought when I signed the deal, but once the process started I found myself rewriting huge chunks of the manuscript. The American writer, James Michener once said, "I am not a very good writer, but I am an excellent rewriter." My patience was severely tested over several months as my manuscript underwent multiple revisions and countless edits.

And then the day arrived when my book was finally published and became available in bookstores. I mistakenly thought that my work had ended, blissfully unaware that it had just begun. Very few writers realize that they need to play a more active and vigorous role in marketing, publicizing and distributing their books. Why should a publisher care about your title if you don't? Around 90,000 books are published in India each year. Ninety percent of books published in the country sell less than 2,000 units per year.

When I began making the rounds of bookstores, I was sorely disappointed to find that my title was hard to find. Bookstores had very little inventory. If it all they did, my book was not visible. Over the next few months, I made it my mission to visit every key store in every town that I visited and ensure that I met with the sales manager or bookstore owner. A personal interaction ensured that their interest in the book went beyond the initial order and sure enough, my sales began to register an upward tick. In the meantime one of the first newspaper reviews appeared and it was outstanding. I breathed easy after a long time.

It has now been a decade (and ten books) since my first novel was published but today I have a better understanding of the term 'bloody good luck'. Bloody good luck is not manna from the heavens. It is the conscious product of five important inputs. These are Passion, Patience, Persistence, Positivity and Perseverance. Let me briefly explain what they mean in the context of the world of writing.

1. Passion: If you are passionate about what you write, your work will resonate with your readers. Don't try to be someone else.
2. Patience: The world of publishing works slowly. Remaining patient is a key ingredient in seeing through your project to fruition.
3. Persistence: There are going to be failures along the way. The real failure is not getting back on your feet after a setback.
4. Positivity: If I had allowed the first negative review to disillusion me, I would never have made it to the next one that was glowing.
5. Perseverance: One more rewrite will not kill you. One more bookstore visit cannot hurt. Stay the course and you will see results eventually.

There is no shortcut to success. Ernest Hemmingway supposedly said, 'Write drunk, edit sober.' My own mantra is slightly different. It goes something like this:

Write when drunk
Edit when sober
Persevere and persist
That's the hangover

Ashwin Sanghi ranks among India's highest selling English fiction authors. He has written several bestsellers (The Rozabal Line, Chanakya's Chant, The Krishna Key, The Sialkot Saga, Keepers of the Kalachakra) and two New York Times bestselling crime thrillers with James Patterson, Private India (sold in the US as City on Fire) and Private Delhi (sold in the US as Count to Ten). Included by Forbes India in their Celebrity 100 and winner of the Crossword Popular Choice, Ashwin has also mentored, co-written and edited titles in the immensely popular 13 Steps series.

Do Writers Make Money?:
Durjoy Datta

LET'S GET some depressing facts out of the way. If you're a new author you can expect to have a first print run of 2000 copies. This means that you can expect to get paid an advance between Rs 20,000-40,000. No, this is not a typo. And no, I haven't missed an extra zero or two. This is the reality. To make things worse, you can't expect much even from your royalties. A new author's book will either not be reprinted or will see a poor reprint. Therefore, almost 90% of new authors cannot expect to make more than Rs 50,000 in total from their first book! When you take into consideration that you can spend 1-1.5 years writing a book, six months bringing out a book, and an infinite amount of time marketing your book, the return on investment on your time is poor. Like I said earlier, it's depressing.

In India no one—expect maybe Chetan Bhagat and Amish—can be full-time writers. In my opinion, Amish and Chetan are the only ones who can get by easily with enough earning potential for the next 10 years. Other bestselling writers like Preeti Shenoy, Ravinder and I can sustain right now (but it's possible that we might not earn enough if the market shifts), while for other authors it's much less. Frankly, even I was a full time novelist for only one year. I worked with an engineering firm. I did my MBA. I had a management job. I setup my own publishing house. And I worked for TV. Like India's other bestselling authors (Amish, Chetan and Ravinder Singh), I've also done my MBA, yet the truth is that by the time my colleagues hit 40 they'll be earning more than I will. This is why someone like Ravi Subramanian, who is the top-most guy in his company, won't leave his job to become a full-time writer. This is because you cannot expect to pay rent or even the electricity bill with a writing income.

Choosing to write full-time also depends on your background. For engineering or management graduates who are from premier institutes, it doesn't make economic sense. For other careers, it might, but only barely.

There are four mediums in which you can be a writer: TV, journalism, books, and movies. Movies present the same scenario as books, where only the top 5-6 writers can eke a living out of writing. But TV has a host of people who earn a lot of money. Even assistant writers stand to earn a lot, so for me, personally, writing for TV is a safe choice. Every month I have a target of writing say 22 episodes, which gives me a safety net. It also helps that in TV writing I'm not the only stakeholder, unlike in books where the author stands to gain or lose the most from the book's success or failure. The best thing about TV writing is that I don't have to care about how much my book has sold! I write better when I know that I'm getting a monthly cheque from another job. I can write without the pressure and worry about sales targets or new book deadlines. It takes a load off my chest.

I often get asked whether a writer can make money from speaking engagements. Yes, a lot of us get a lot of invitations to go to colleges and conferences to talk. But sadly it is rare to get a paid engagement. This only happens if you have some crazy fans, or a rich college or sponsor. Most often speaking engagements mean we end up wasting a day without getting anything in return. Unless all writers decide to stand in unity not to speak for free, you can't bank on getting paid for speaking engagements. You can't rely on making money off this. If it comes it comes.

This is the same with brand endorsements. Sometimes a few brands like to have authors represent them, but this is not a reliable or steady source of income. And it is definitely not the norm! Brands collaborating with micro-celebrities, like bestselling authors, are a new phenomenon, since it's normally TV and movie stars who endorse products. Of course, my day gets made when a brand approaches me. It's like Diwali! It's exciting and surprising to make such easy money! Brands look at the social media profile of an influencer to decide what to pay them to promote their products and to push for certain experiences. There are caveats, of course. Sometimes I get stuck whether to put up posts that I personally like, or posts that will click with brands. Sometimes it gets annoying for my followers if I push too many products or brands, or push the brands too often. Sometimes I get paid to endorse brands that I would've endorsed even if they'd just sent me a sample of their product! The truth is that if you tell any writer that 'we'll put you on TV', they will not even ask you for money!

But brand gigs are rare for authors. Remember, for anyone to know you as a writer they have to spend money (to buy your book), *and* take out an entire day to read your book. It's not the same with other influencers, like say comedians, where the content is online and the laughter is free.

Sadly, over the last few years, things haven't gotten better for authors in the publishing industry. The advances and royalties remain the same as they were ten years ago. This is because while it's easier to get published, it's not easier to get readers. It's also difficult for a new writer to make a mark. In commercial fiction, at least, the same 5-6 top writers have been circulating for the last ten years. With literary books it's even tougher to sell, and your focus as a literary author should be on earning awards and getting traction outside India.

To sum it up, don't get carried away with the false notion of becoming rich writing books! Even if you're a bestselling author, don't quit your job! If you want to be a novelist who wants to tell stories, and you're unable to maintain a full-time job, then look at jobs where you can write, like TV or movies, where there's some connection to your passion. If you love writing you will find time for it even with a full-time job.

Durjoy Datta is one of India's top bestselling novelists. He is also a screenwriter with award-winning shows written for Channel V India, Sony TV and Star Plus. He served at NIIT Ltd. Siemens AG, and American Express until he co-founded the publishing house Grapevine India in 2011. In 2009, The Times of India recognized him as a young achiever. Whistling Woods International also chose him as one of the two young achievers in the field of Media and Communications in 2011. In 2012, he was one of the recipients of the Teacher's Achievement Awards. He has spoken at various TEDx conferences for colleges across India.

How To Market Your Book: Ravi Subramanian

OVER THREE millions books are brought out every year. The reader has limited time and the choice is mind-boggling. On top of that, readers today are well-set with their own choice of authors. How do you dismantle one of those authors from the "to-read" list of your reader, and get into that list instead? By marketing your book. This helps you make inroads into the readers mindspace, and enables you to get into his consideration subset. A number of brilliant books don't get read because the reader does not even know of the book's existence! Marketing a book ensures that your book does not become one of those.

You can't hope to rely solely on your publisher to promote your book. Comitment to marketing varies form publisher to publisher. However, remember that for all publishers, publishing is a business. It has to make commercial sense. So don't expect too much spend from them on marketing. Also, for the publisher your book is one of many, whereas for you it is the ONLY ONE. Hence, unless you are a bestseller, no publisher will go out of the way to maket a book. My advice—stop expecting the publisher to do things for you, do it yourself. You will be at peace.

These days most sucessful authors spend a lot of time creating a brand and marketing themselves. A release of a book is an event around which the entire marketing and branding activity peaks. It is important for a successful author to be seen and heard throughout the year and not just around the time of release of a book. In short, being an author is a full time job, even when you are not writing a book.

Many bestselling authors embark on the journey of promoting their book, much before they have even written it. They draw the reader in at every stage and create excitement about what is in store. Be it a title reveal, cover reveal, publishing process, naming characters etc, they involve the reader. They create sharable content on social media. Most importantly they engage with their readers throughout the year and not only around the time of a book release. They make the readers a part of their extended family.

It's not even about the money, but about creating a lingering, longlasting and impactful message. Social media allows one to do this at a reasonable cost. I would say that if authors want to make a definitive impact, they need to approach the 'marketing of books' as a startup. In any business, you would plough back all that you earn into building your business. The same holds for books. When you are starting on this journey, make sure that you do not blow up all your money on frivolous dinners, glitzy parties, and designer clothing. Instead spend it on creating a visibility for the book and a brand for the author. That will stand you in good stead.

New authors need to make sure that they are seen. That's the first step to marketing a book. Getting paid visibility is very expensive. So while they go about pushing the publisher to make sure the book is available at all distribution points, they need to make use of every opportunity to gain visibility—lit fests, book events, talks, college visits, club tie-ups, they need to do everything which is possible. Readers are more likely to buy books by authors they have interacted with. That said, nothing beats a well-written book. So your first priority should be to write a good book.

Being a good storyteller is a must for being on the bestseller list. Every other aspect of the book can be corrected and set right by a team of good editors. But no one can fix a storytelling flaw. You can either get into the reader's mind and tell him a story, or allow him access to yours and tell him a story. Irrespective of what your story telling approach is, you need to make sure that the story is relevant and interesting to the reader. Often this is where many authors stumble. What is exciting for the author may be drab for the reader. Figuring this out and understanding this gap goes a long way in your quest to write an Indian bestseller.

A good promotion campaign may create a certain hype around a book and help it sell. Controversies may play a similar role. All I can say is that a good campaign can make a reader buy a book, but it can never make him or her fall in love with it.

Another quick point. There are a number of good and successful women authors across the world. Some of the best books, across genres, have been penned by women. There would be more women dominating the word of writing, but for their hesitation in promoting themselves and their work. Often, they worry about people around them judging them by the book they write and stay away. I can confirm that in India the best writing comes from the women authors that we have. They shouldn't hesitate, at all, to market their books!

The best advice I can give authors is: don't follow trends. Write what you feel like writing. Just because it's the season of romances, don't write romance. Unless you write from the bottom of your heart and are passionate about what you write, you will never be succeesssful. If you look at all the big authors—both Indian and international—one thing stands out: they did not time the market. They were all trendsetters in their own way.

A banker by profession, Ravi Subramanian has written popular thrillers about banking and bankers, including the award-winning trilogy The Incredible Banker, The Bankster and Bankerupt.

How To Use Social Media To Promote Your Books: Kiran Manral

I OWE being an author to social media. Cross my heart. It all began with blogging. I quit full time work when my son was born, but the itchy fingers wouldn't stop and I began blogging about being a parent. The mommy blogger universe back then was nurturing and supportive, and the anecdotes I posted about raising the offspring got me a sizeable following. With that came the exhortations from friends to write a book. And so, a year before I turned forty, I bit the bullet and wrote my first book. I was lucky enough to get signed up by the first editor I sent it out to, and there began my journey as an author.

Because I came into the publishing world, having built up—over a period of almost six years—a definite audience who had already read my writing and knew what to expect, marketing my first book was a matter of reaching out to this audience and letting them know that I'd written a book. They were kind and gracious, and became my online cheerleading group: generously hosting me and my new book on their blogs, writing reviews of my books, carrying interviews, and spreading word of mouth. I didn't use social media to promote my first book, as much as social media graciously opened its arms and did all it could to spread the word about my book. Which brings me to the lessons in promoting one's book via social media:

Lesson Number One: It's all about relationships. No one will post about your book unless, a) you're a friend, or someone they've had some kind of positive interaction with, or b) they really really like your book, or c) you've paid them to do so. Ideally, if you're not going to be doing c) and are not relying on the b), it is a) that you want to leverage. Therefore, build great networks on social media. This is not popping in a couple of times a day onto your twitter feed, peering around, blinking, spouting wisdom from your soap box, and getting off. This means interactions, finding your tribe, building it, being a support to other authors, retweeting stuff they post about their books and creating good karma. Twitter is a two-way conversation. You cannot use twitter like a billboard.

Lesson Number Two: Ensure that you have a presence on all social media, but use them as per the medium they are for. Blogs and Twitter are words. Instagram, Pinterest and Facebook are primarily visuals. YouTube, Vine, etc are videos. Create content that works across all social media, for example, a quick video of you talking about your book can go across all platforms. Remember, visual posts, images and videos get greater traction than large chunks of text. Rather ironic when we're trying to sell a book. Don't use every single post to promote yourself or your book. Build yourself into a domain expert, talk about your expertise, encourage dialogue and reaction. Also, don't be on social media too much (some absence is always good to make sure you don't become a blind spot on the timeline to your followers). Create a launch event on FB, a cover reveal, invite your friends and family to it. Do a Facebook live at the launch, have a reading, and take questions. Use Instagram live whenever you visit bookstores or do book reading events. Use Google Hangouts to take questions from readers. Offer a free writing workshop online for aspiring authors. Create goodwill.

Lesson Number Three: Create giveaways. Everybody loves free stuff. Sometimes you can give away your book. At other times, you can create a contest around your book and then give away stuff. Create a hashtag, preferably the title of your book for easy recall, and have folks you know talk about it on their social media. Use platforms like Goodreads to create giveaways of your book. A huge mistake I made was sending out copies to all and sundry with the initial books, which was a huge investment in terms of buying copies and investing in courier charges. Now as I'm older and wiser, and tighter fisted, I don't do that anymore. Most people don't even acknowledge receiving a copy, leave alone talk about the book. I would rather do giveaways on various reading groups and send out copies to folks who show any interest in reading the books. Do giveaways on your Facebook page, on your Twitter feed, on your Instagram. Have folks tag other folks to get your message amplified. Signed copy giveaways are always great.

Lesson Number Four: Don't shy away from paid promotions, whether it's Facebook Ads, Twitter promotions or blog tours. All the ways to reach out to your audience can only amplify your reach for your book. I haven't personally used these, I must confess, but friends I know have recommended these very strongly.

Lesson Number Five: Use newsletters to keep your readers informed about book releases, giveaways, and book reading events. Build up a database of email addresses of readers, and keep sending them regular mail updates. Be respectful in your emails though, put your information across, don't be a mail spammer, and collect emails to build up your database. I used MailChimp for the longest while to send out emails about my new releases.

And finally, above all, build your word of mouth on a great product. All the marketing means nothing if people don't genuinely have good things to say about your book. Invest more time and effort in writing your book than promoting it.

God knows, I was the Energizer Bunny of promoting my books on social media initially, but now I am jaded and believe that the only promotion worth it is word-of-mouth. If you've cracked that, you've got it made.

An award-winning author, TEDx speaker, columnist and mentor, Kiran Manral has been in various avatars, a journalist, India culture lead and trend spotter, qualitative market researcher and is currently Ideas Editor with a women centric news portal. She was awarded the Women Achievers Award by Young Environmentalists Association in 2014, the WOW Award in 2016, was shortlisted for the Femina Women Awards for Literary Contribution in 2017. The Indian Council of UN Relations (ICUNR) supported by the Ministry for Women and Child Development, Government of India, awarded her the International Women's Day Award 2018 for excellence in the field of writing.

How To Write A Book Review:
Vivek Tejuja

Here's a step-by-step guide on how to write a good book review:

1. Read the damn book. If you don't read the book cover to cover, please do not attempt to write the review. It will show. Not in the first review. Nor in the second. In the hundredth, for sure.

2. Understand the book. Don't read the synopsis, because it's there. Read, read, and read to understand what's being said. After all, you have to include it in the review. Look for what the author is trying to say at various points in the book to be able to project that in your review.

3. Please do not use adjectives for the sake of using them. Use them because you actually loved the book and not because you want to make an author or a publisher happy. Reviewers often fall into this trap and then it becomes quite difficult to get out of it.

4. Don't try and make the review unnecessarily long. If you think you have said what you had to, then end the review. It is all right. There is no set word-count in the land of reviewers, which if you do not adhere to, you will be flogged.

5. What did you feel while reading the book? Always ask yourself this question while writing the review and be honest about the answer. Don't be a wuss and give in to praising the book without reason.

6. You do not have to get personal toward the author. Be objective. Stick to the book.

7. Also, not directly related to this, but stick to timelines. If you have committed a review on a particular date, please deliver. Or face the collective wrath of the God of Reading (there is one, trust me).

8. Again, a little unrelated: Do not pose as a reviewer only because you want free books. While it's great that you want to read, do actually read the titles that you ask for. Don't let them gather dust.

9. Be amicable. Do not get nasty just because an author said something you did not like, or if a publisher isn't entertaining your review requests. It is all right. They do not owe you anything.

And now, a special announcement for dear authors.

Dear authors,

1. Learn how to take criticism. Trust me it does not hurt all that much. The boo-boo will go away soon enough.

2. Please do not ask reviewers to justify their review. It's in very poor taste, isn't it?

3. Do not message reviewers on every platform asking them to review your book. If they don't want to and are unable to say that, get the message and move on.

Finding book reviews in newspapers today is literally like searching for a needle in a haystack. Online, on the other hand, there are a dime a dozen reviews, most of which don't even whet the appetite. There are Instagrammers (nothing to say here), YouTubers or BookTubers (really now) to be precise, and people who review books in 280 characters. I, for one, depend solely on sites such as Lit Hub, or *The Guardian* and *The New York Times*, to help me make the decision to buy or not to buy.

Last, but not the least, a review is just an opinion. And, a personal one at that. It should not cloud anyone's judgement to read or not read a particular book. If you want to, by all means go ahead and read a book. A review is just an enabler and should be nothing more.

Besides being a bibliophile, Vivek Tejuja loves food and his two cats. An accidental writer, he indulges and wishes there was more time to write and read. A Bombay boy through and through, the sea is one of his loves. Men are also a part of his existence on and off. So Now You Know is Vivek's debut book, released by Penguin in October 2018.

How To Be A Successful Poet:
Arundhathi Subramaniam

FIRST THINGS first. If you nurse dreams of owning a corpulent bank balance and posing for selfie-gatherers and autograph hunters, turn this page. Or turn to fiction. Or better still, turn Bollywood lyricist.

The reasons not to be an Anglophone Indian poet are legion. Publishers are few and far between, royalties are meager, and readers sparse. An American survey even claims that poets die sooner than other species of writers! (Not surprising given the seemingly terminal levels of inaudibility.)

On one level, admittedly, things seem to be looking up. Smaller publishers are making their presence felt. Larger publishers are reviving their poetry agendas. Performance poetry has turned glamorous. And the online scene is simply crackling with activity: whether it's poets, poet aspirants or poetasters, the whole world seems to be in cyberia!

And yet, poetry sales remain modest. Although everyone has written at least one bad teenage love poem, it is truly confounding how no one grows up to become a reader, much less a buyer. Someone once said writing poetry is like throwing a petal down the Grand Canyon and waiting for an echo. It's as absurd as that.

But oddly, echoes do happen. Subtle echoes. Intangible echoes. And being a successful poet is to know that the subtlest rewards are the deepest.

External odds notwithstanding, the real challenge for the poet is internal. Heightened emotion isn't enough. A burning message to convey to the world isn't enough. Mere dexterity with language isn't enough. Making poetry is a demanding business. How does one combine form and content, craft and creativity, rigour and rasa, precision and passion, artistry and authenticity? How does one create that slippery, elusive beast called a poem?

Through my adolescence and twenties, I underwent long periods of apprenticeship, conscious and unconscious. There were spells of what I now call "séance" when the voices of poets I didn't particularly care for seemed to speak through me. There were spells of "ventriloquism" when other poets seemed to write what I thought of as *my* poem (which made me writhe in envy). There were also spells of laryngitis when I had no voice at all.

Then there were the strident voices of the cultural climate, voices that decreed how to be postcolonial, how to be a woman, how to be modern, how to be traditional, how to be political. (Years later, this prompted my spluttering rage poem against glib identity politics: 'To the Welsh Critic Who Doesn't Find Me Identifiably Indian').

In short, the challenges were for real. I knew poetry could never be a career, a livelihood. But I was beginning to realise that it was one hell of an exacting vocation.

Gradually, I began to arrive at my own definition of success. Success, I decided, was, quite simply, about growing into the best possible version of myself. That threatened to be a lifelong journey. But it seemed worth it. And still does. Being a successful poet, I decided, was to find a voice that was the truest and best possible version of my own, and trusting that it was capable of touching others. It worked. The less I bothered about being recognized, the more I grew into myself. And paradoxically, that's when my poems seemed to touch readers more deeply as well.

Looking back, if I had to distill my journey into a few guidelines, here's what they'd be.

1. **Read:** It's truly amazing how many write poetry, but never bother to read, leave alone buy, the work of contemporary poets. If you want to know your milieu, to hone your craft, if you want to be read, read others. Above all, if you claim to love poetry, *read*. Read widely, read deeply, read generously.

2. **Revise:** Spontaneous overflows of powerful feeling are important. But crafting, tweaking, revising and reworking are as vital. The best poets know that inspiration and perspiration go together. Magic and manual labour are inseparable.

3. **Take Your Time:** It doesn't matter if A has a mediocre book that everyone's gushing over, or if B's posted Facebook photos of himself quaffing wine with Gulzar. Races are for rodents. Trust the process. Don't be in a hurry to declare yourself a genius. Successful poets don't arrive. They're always still getting there. A sound first step would be to send a poem or two to literary journals. (You'll find names and addresses online.) When you have a substantial collection of poems published in journals, you could start thinking of a manuscript. Send drafts around to writer friends you trust. Mull over their feedback. If their responses resonate with hunches you have about what might be the problem with a text, take them seriously. Finally, after you're convinced you can stand by every word and hyphen in your manuscript, start contacting publishers.

4. **Don't Turn Clone:** Successful poets walk their own path and sing their own tune. Don't turn performance poet because someone tells you it's cool. Let your temperament decide whether you're meant for the megaphone or the murmur. Most importantly, don't try to be someone else. Don't try to become a Szymborska, a Walcott or a Kolatkar. Find out what it means to be *you*.

5. **Don't Turn Networking Fiend:** There's a new brand of poet with business cards and manuscripts that strides around lit fests, only acknowledging the existence of publishers, agents,

curators or potential blurb/review writers. Don't allow yourself to be infected by the self-promotion brigade. Real poets are always good listeners, seldom good broadcasters.

6. **Don't Let Your Inner Demagogue Dictate The Kind Of Poetry You Write:** Social media networks offer encouragement, but often turn into fiestas of self-congratulation. Beware of the easy pat on the back. Subtext and suggestion are the terrain of poetry. Remember: the hushed voice can be quietly radical, the whisper subversive, the pause devastating.

7. **Keep The Spirit Of Self-Criticism Alive:** A local writers' group can do wonders. Be supportive but critical of each other, and make sure that the community doesn't turn coterie. Examine line lengths, wonder about verbs, argue about adjectives. Robust workshop criticism can elevate even a middling poem to another level. (A word of warning: constructive self-criticism is not corrosive self-doubt. Stay receptive to feedback, but stay away from the naysayers.)

8. **Celebrate:** Remember, real poets take poetry seriously, not themselves. Being successful is about knowing that there are no VIPs here. Enjoy your inconsequentiality. Celebrate it. Therein lies your freedom.

Arundhathi Subramaniam is an award-winning poet whose recent book, When God is a Traveller, *was shortlisted for the prestigious TS Eliot Prize and won the inaugural Khushwant Singh Prize and Il Ceppo Award. Described as 'one of the finest poets writing in India today' (The Hindu, 2010), she has been widely translated and anthologised. As editor, her books include the acclaimed anthology of Bhakti poetry,* Eating God. *She is also a performing arts curator, critic and prose writer on Indian spirituality.*

The Art Of Translation:
Arunava Sinha

THE TIME has come for Indian publishing to have presses dedicated to publishing translated literature. For books that are translated into English from other Indian languages, to begin with, followed by translations of books between different non-English Indian languages. Contrary to popular perception, the heavyweights of Indian publishing—in almost any language, barring, arguably, Malayalam—are no longer engaged or even invested in publishing translated literature. Most of the major as well as smaller publishers have reduced the number of books in translation that they publish. This is particularly felt in the area of serious fiction, which is the category of translated books that was thriving even five or six years ago.

Some of this paling of the passion for translated literature can be placed within a general narrowing of interest in publishing serious fiction. Under pressure to shore up their top and bottomlines in a market where there no longer seem to be enough readers for novels and short stories meant to engage the mind, most presses have cut down on the number of such titles, preferring to rely on already established writers when it comes to this particular category. In contrast, one of the prime motives behind publishing translated literature is to introduce writers who are new to the language they are being translated into.

That is how the most famous writers not writing in English were published in translation in the Anglophone world. And that is how many writers in Tamil and Malayalam, Bengali and Kannada, Hindi and Urdu, Gujarati and Rajasthani, Odia and Assamese, were published in English in India as well.

But that golden period seems to be ending. As business-led circumspection overtakes the impulse to publish books that will last for decades, as the need to bring out titles with immediate box-office appear overrides the mission of creating a reading list for not just the present but also the future, publishers in India are left with only a token footprint in the space, almost as if to be able to claim, 'We also publish translations'. It is not just a question of the numbers. Were an established publisher to bring out, say, no more than half a dozen translated works a year, but accord to each of them the lavish attention that such a book needs and deserves, that would have done justice to those titles. But as things stand, publishing these translations have turned into a nod to something like corporate social responsibility, a checking of the 'translation' box, and little more.

As the big publishing houses, most of them multinationals, lift their feet off the accelerator for translation, some of the smaller presses are stepping up to fill the gap. Unfortunately, their intent is not matched by their execution. Publishing translations is a tricky business, starting with the decision of what to publish. In India, the process usually originates with the translator, since editors at publishing companies are not familiar with the different literatures of the country, except, in some cases, those in their mother tongue. So, it is up to the translator to double as scout and agent in identifying books worthy of translation and then pitching them. Unlike with Western publishing companies, the process is not particularly rigorous: there is no methodical journey through synopsis and samples, attention to canons, an understanding of the writer's reputation and provenance, or polling readers for responses. As a result, translations are often published on faith, even by the major publishers, and on the assumption that the translator has chosen well. Naturally, the smaller publishers are not rigorous either. Nor do all of them have editors who have both the ability and the experience to turn a good translation into a fine one— or even to reject a mediocre translation, which is often replete with poor use of language, tone-deaf rendition, and an utter inability to go beyond the meanings of the words.

What is to be done, then? When I began translating Bengali fiction—and, later, poetry and non-fiction—into English a little over 10 years ago, publishing firms like Penguin Books, Random House (they had not yet merged), HarperCollins, and Hachette, to name but four, had already discovered the potential of publishing translations. Unlike books written originally in English, these were tried and tested works in their original language, having met with both popular and critical acclaim. These publishers nurtured the books, marketed them with attention and finesse, and carried the titles beyond their being published to ensure that they found readers. That has changed drastically. Publishers are focussed on big books (read: those written by celebrities or those with instant appeal, preferably both), and translated books in particular die in infancy, before they can even make it into the hands of readers. With bookshops dwindling in number, discovery of translated books is well-nigh possible, and few even come to know of the existence of these translations, unless the writer and translator are willing to hustle them on social media. Not even that can ensure more than the instant karma of likes, seldom translating into actual purchases.

To be sure, publishers like Oxford University Press, Seagull Books, Neogy Books, and a few others are actually looking to publish more translations. But they are swimming valiantly upstream, while the tide sweeps towards the "market" and the "target reader", those dreaded words for translators. Even at the best of times, no one could make a living out of translating literary fiction—which is true around the world as well, for all but those at the very top of the profession—in India. Now, advances against royalties, the usual form of compensation for the work already done in the process of translating a book, are going south alarmingly, with the result that six months' effort does not even earn a week's salary when compared to, say, a job in publishing (which is not the highest paid line of work to begin with).

Paradoxically, this downshift has come at a time when writers in Indian languages are extremely keen on being translated. Unlike the generation that preceded them, whose members were often content with the success of their books in their original languages, today's younger writer is seeking a wider national and international readership. They are more than interested in collaborating with translators. But the mainstream publishers no longer go beyond the classics and the handful of established writers in each non-English Indian language when it comes to translations. The timing of this shrinking interest couldn't be more ironic, for there are now several literary prizes in India that books translated into English are eligible to win. The Crossword Translation Award, the Muse India Translation Award and the Sahitya Akademi translations awards are exclusive to this category. In addition, translated books can compete alongside those written in English for the lucrative JCB Prize, the DSC Prize, and, now, the Hindu Prize.

If this paints a less than shining picture for translations into English, the situation is even more dire for translations between other Indian languages. Some people still recall a time when, for instance, readers in languages ranging from Gujarati to Telugu, from Hindi to Tamil, would not believe that Sarat Chandra Chattopadhyay—a Bengali writer—was in fact translated, so steeped were they in his works. The finest literature was translated freely between Indian languages, and readers around the country had the benefit of reading the Indian canon in their mother tongue, no matter which language a work had originally been written in. Today, there are not even translators between several pairs of languages. A Tamil publisher told me recently that he has not had a request in over twenty years for any of his works to be translated into Bengali. Regional literatures—with, perhaps, the notable exception of Malayalam—are increasingly turning insular and market-facing, unwilling to experiment with translated works from other parts of India. And the Mcdonaldisation of popular culture is forcing readers towards an anodyne form of fiction written in English, devoid of the strengths and uniqueness of the literatures written in other languages and in regions outside the big cities.

What is to be done, then? There has never been a better time, in fact, for India to have its own translation presses. Presses like In Other Words, Portobello Books, Tilted Axis, and Fitzcarraldo Editions, among others, are already showing the way to this in the UK, as are Archipelago Press, Dalkey Archives, New Directions, and Open Letter Books in the US. In India, much of Seagull Books' publications are works in translation, not just from Indian languages, but from those around the world. What do these presses bring to the table? For one thing, they were aware—and proud—of the fact that they spearhead a disruption of the market for literature. Translations disrupt existing structures, expectations, cultural constructs, narrative experiences and even the economics of publishing in a way that big presses, intent on monetising formulaic books, not only abhor but also resent. Firms that publish for a market try to guess what readers want. Translation presses, on the other hand, give readers what they had no idea could exist in the form of books. They continuously disturb the status quo, and form new tastes instead of reinforcing old ones. Moreover, they own their translated books well beyond the act of getting them out of the printing presses. They champion these titles, they take them to reviewers and influencers, they guide them into the hands of intrepid readers, all the while subverting existing ways of making and selling books.

For translation to find the place that it deserves in India, for the multiple literatures of the country to find their way into the hands of people everywhere, for a diversity of literary voices to be heard loud and clear, especially in these times when there are attempts to force-feed everyone a single narrative in a single language, it is necessary for translation presses to spring up. It is axiomatic that no one but readers can finance such presses. India lacks a thoughtful arts or literature council with an appreciation of diversity, India's corporations are almost without exception interested in showbiz rather than literature when it comes to the arts, and individual philanthropists care more for technology than they do for creative work. But no matter. For translation presses can bring about a reading revolution in India, and where there is a revolution, there will always be life.

Arunava Sinha translates classic, modern and contemporary Bengali fiction and non-fiction into English. Over 40 of his translations have been published so far, and he has won several awards in India for translated books, besides having his works on the longlists and shortlists of international prizes for translations. Besides India, his translations have been published in the UK and the US in English, and in several European and Asian countries through further translation. He was born and grew up in Kolkata, and lives and writes in New Delhi.

How *Not* To Write Children's Books: Anushka Ravishankar

IT IS a notion universally held that anyone who has ever met a child can write for children. So you have people writing in to children's publishers saying, 'I have written this story for my grandson, my niece, my son, my friend's daughter's best friend ...'! No children's publisher wants to hear this.

Children's publishers are engaged in the serious business of creating literature for children. Some of them create picture books, some chapter books and some of them publish the whole range. In India, you have the big players—Penguin Random House and Harper Collins, which have children's imprints; and Scholastic that publishes exclusively for children. And you have a number of exciting independent publishers—Tara Books, Karadi Tales, Tulika Books, Duckbill Books, Pickle Yolk and Talking Cub, to name just a few.

So, if you want to embark on a career of writing for children, you should do your research and figure out who publishes what. Sending a YA novel to a publisher who does only picture books would be a waste of everyone's time!

But before you start, ask yourself: is this what you really want to do? In my experience, writing for children is fun and addictive, but what it's not is lucrative. Nor is it prestigious. So if you're in it for the lucre or the fame, run! Write for adults (maybe) or better still, get into the Italian-leather-buying business. I've heard there's a lot of money in it. And if it's fame you crave, become a film star. Or a cricketer.

If after all this, you still want to write for kids (Are you sure? Really?), then you need to know how. There are no rules, but there are some things that are good to keep in mind.

Writing for children is as easy or difficult as writing for adults, with one added complication: you are writing for and about a group of people that you're not a part of. But, fortunately, as a writer for children, you can't be accused of appropriation. Not just because no one listens to children (this is sad, even criminal, but true), but because if you are an adult, you've already been a child. It amazes me how people seem to forget that.

As a children's writer, that's an important, even essential memory to have. If you remember what it was like to be a child, then you will automatically write as and for that child. The questions of audience and readership and age-appropriateness become moot. All you need to do is go back to how you felt at that age. It's really an extension of that one quality that no writer can do without: empathy.

As an adult setting out to write a story for children, one is inclined to think: what can I teach them through this story? Can I teach them about a new place? Can I teach them the value of goodness, concern for the environment, the importance of reading?

That's what a teacher does—looks for lessons in everything. And yes, children need good teachers. But we are not teachers. As writers of fiction, our primary loyalty should be to the story. If the story teaches good values, new things, introduces new people, then good for it. But if it doesn't, well, too bad; that's really not our job.

Our question to ourselves should only be: does this story engage the child, does it grab her and take her on an adventure? And at the end of the adventure, one hopes the child comes out a bit wiser, happier, more sensitive ... but that's a by-product; collateral benefit, if you will.

The writer's job is to make that journey compelling; through action, through the people we populate the adventure with, through humour, perhaps, and through the best possible use of our words.

So, here are my five commandments for writing for children:

THOU SHALT NOT PREACH. Of course you can talk about serious things or take a stand about things. But do this without preaching, please. A storybook should be an escape from the tyranny of the power of adults, not a sneaky way for adults to preach some more to the hapless mites!

THOU SHALT NOT TALK DOWN. Who do you write for? When you're writing for adults, this question does not come up. You are writing for yourself. If you like horror, that's what you write. If you like romance, then you write that. But when you're writing for a child, you tend to try and write for some amorphous mass of 'childness', which does not exist. That's when you end up talking down to your reader.

THOU SHALT NOT SIMPLIFY. Don't obsess about 'appropriate vocabulary'. Children will read what delights and excites them, even if they don't understand every word. The joy of reading is closely connected to the joy of language. If you deny yourself the joy of using the best word in a sentence, you're denying that joy to the reader as well.

Salman Rushdie said it perfectly: 'It's fun to read things when you don't know all the words. Even children love it. One of the things any great children's writer will tell you is that children like it if in books designed for their age group there is a vocabulary just slightly bigger than theirs. So they come up against weird words, and the weird words excite them. If you describe a small girl in a story as "loquacious," it works so much better than "talkative." And then some little girl will read the book and her sister will be shooting her mouth off and she will say to her sister, "Don't be so *loquacious*." It is a whole new weapon in her arsenal.'

THOU SHALT NOT BE UNFUNNY. It's not absolutely necessary to make your reader laugh; not all books are meant to be funny. But even a serious story can be written with a light and humorous touch. Having said that, there's nothing as satisfying as making your reader laugh. And if you can make a child laugh, that is a special joy.

THOU SHALT NOT BE BORING. Does this need an explanation? If you bore the child, he will close the book and go out to play. As he should. A book must be a thing of joy—you can't force a child to read for the sake of self-improvement (this stops no one from doing exactly that). So don't complain that children aren't reading. Make your book exciting enough and children will want to read it!

Anushka Ravishankar has written over thirty-five books for children, including picture books in verse, chapter books, retellings of folk tales and non-fiction. Several of them have been published internationally and have won awards. In 2012, she co-founded Duckbill Books, which publishes funny, edgy and exciting Indian books for children and young adults.

How To Publish From Remote Parts Of India: Jacinta Kerketta

I AM an adivasi (tribal) writer who belongs to a village called Khudposh in Jharkhand. I grew up seeing my mother beaten up by my policeman father. I saw my village go from a Maoist 'liberated zone' to a site of intense conflict over its forest and mineral wealth. I saw my uncle and his mother pulled out from the fields one day and killed due to a land dispute with a powerful non-tribal family. The struggle of my family echoed in my heart and became a voice.

I did not grow up with money or any access to the world of publishing. But I used to love writing, whether it was short stories or poems. In class VIII I heard of a magazine called *Rahi* that was based in the capital city of Ranchi. I wanted to send them my work but did not have the money for stamps or envelopes. My class teacher, Sr Lucia, paid out-of-pocket for my work to be sent. Every month my work would be published in the magazine, along with those of other children from around India. We all became pen friends. All this was very thrilling.

I began to write poems about violence against women, hunger, government apathy to tribal regions and displacement, but I had no idea where I could send them for publication. So I started posting them on Facebook and they were widely shared. One day I met Professor Shriprakash Shukla of Benares Hindu

University in Ranchi and read him my poems. He published them in BHU's literary magazine *Parichay*. Later five of my poems were published in the literary magazine *Naya Jnanodaya* from Delhi, with a special commentary from the editor Leeladhar Mandloi.

I was then invited by well-known Jharkhandi documentary filmmaker Meghnath to read some of my poems at a program in Odisha that had been organised by the German Adivasi Coordination Committee. There I met Johannes Laping, a German translator who had translated several novels of Mahasweta Devi into German, and established a publishing house named Draupadi Verlag in Germany that focussed on Indian literature. In March 2016, Draupadi Verlag published my first collection of poems in Hindi and German under the title of *Glut*.

In the same year, Adivaani Publishing of Kolkata published the same collection in Hindi and English under the title of *Angor*. *Glut* got re-printed in 2018. Meanwhile, Alessandra Consolaro of Turino University in Italy, whom I had met at Amarkantak University in Madhya Pradesh, translated my entire collection of poems into Italian in a book titled *Brace* that was released during the 31st Turino Book Fair in May 2018. That's when I got the opportunity to do poetry readings in a number of cities and universities across Germany, Italy, Switzerland and Austria, and to talk about the situation of Adivasi people in India.

I never thought that my poems would find their way into the world like this.

People in remote places around India are the original storytellers. The more they struggle with their lives, the more they make the stories of our country come alive. It is very important that they also come into mainstream literature. After all, stories from one particular life are the ones that reach out to the life of others.

So, if you're writing from a village or small town in India, don't be intimidated. Your voice is important. Your work is important.

Young people think that because of their age they do not have sufficient experience to write. Remember, in this world many great works have been created by people who are young, like Karl Marx, Bhagat Singh and many other writers, poets and thinkers. These people have had a great influence on the world. The barrier is in your mind, not in your age, so get over it.

But how can your stories get published and reach people?

While it is difficult to get in touch with great publishers in these times, social media offers you a wide and open platform. Go to publishers' websites and submit your book to them. Good writing will find good publishers. Approach literary magazines. There are many magazines that are searching for young people who write well. They will publish your work on priority. As a new writer you can benefit from such opportunities. Use social media to express yourself, showcase your work and build a loyal base of readers.

Read a lot. Sometimes books don't reach inaccessible places. You can establish contact with energetic people who undertake initiatives like bringing books via say a walking library to remote places.

With all these tools, your urge to write better and self-study will make your writer's point of view stronger and richer.

Whatever you do, don't ever stop writing. Sometimes, those of us who face rejection or don't know how to get published, give up. We stop telling our stories. You don't have to. Today, all over the country, publishing houses wish to publish new young writers. They are asking for manuscripts, they are publishing selected manuscripts, and are even giving awards. All that's important is what you write and the way in which you write it.

Jacinta Kerketta is a young Hindi poet, writer and social worker, who belongs to the Adivasi community of Jharkhand. She has two collections of poems to her credit. In a very short time her books have been published in Hindi, English, German and Italian.

Terribly Tiny Tips On Micro Fiction: Anuj Gosalia

"FOR SALE. Baby shoes. Never worn."

Hemingway is said to have written this powerful six-word story back in the day. So while micro fiction isn't new, it has found a new audience, today. But what does micro fiction entail? Let's find out.

What Is Micro Fiction? Micro fiction is a format in which you write stories that are less than 300 words or take less than 5 minutes to read. At Terribly Tiny Tales, we have a limit of 5,000 characters.

How Do You Write Micro Fiction? One way to approach writing micro fiction is to tell the story that you really want to tell, but write about only the most pivotal moment of that story. Say, for instance, you want to write about your first relationship. If you had to talk about the entire relationship, you'd write a novel, perhaps. But when you're writing a tiny tale, you could write about the time you decided to part ways, or the first kiss, or the silliness of it all. Or you could take the entire relationship and shrink it into a beginning and an end (not much space for a middle, is there?).

In one of the first tales I wrote, I tried to fictionalise an aching memory from a previous relationship. It read:

then i used a feather to write poems on your back,
you wouldn't stop moving.
now i use it as a quill,
not once have my words moved you.

Any Other Writing Hacks? Micro fiction doesn't have the room to establish characters. Therefore, it's important to tell stories that are on relatable topics or have a surprising twist in the end. Ideally, both.

Man walks into a bar.
"Whiskey, large?"
A boy walks out.

Will Writing Micro Fiction Make Me A Bad Writer? Like there are bad novels, the world of micro fiction, because of its accessibility, has a lot of hurried, half-baked writing on display too. But if used well, it can become a valuable tool for a writer. To be able to edit all the fluff even though it came from your genius head, but to still be able to discard it, is a hard but useful skill to grow as a writer.

Who Reads Micro Fiction? In today's times of reducing attention spans (8 seconds at last count), micro fiction has found a massive readership with the always-on mobile folk. These are mostly young people between the ages of 16 and 30, typically in the metro cities of India. But this is slowly changing as regional language storytelling pages and apps have started taking prominence.

Why Does It Work? Most people, thanks to the smartphone, are struggling to finish books. A book, sadly, is a time luxury today. Something you read on a long flight, or on a vacation. That's where micro fiction has found room. It has managed to wriggle into the Uber and metro rides. It has found a home in classroom breaks, and a quick read before sleeping. In fact, social media, especially Instagram, has helped create massive micro fiction and modern poetry influencers in the likes of Rupi Kaur and Lang Leav who are very popular with youngsters across the world.

How Do You Find An Audience? I think it's essential to be consistent on the Internet. The Internet allows you to make mistakes, to grow, and to learn as you evolve. In fact, people prefer to see your raw and imperfect self on social media. Embrace it. Write on topics that you deeply care about, topics that come from an honest place. Seek feedback from readers and writers you find inspiring.

Who Publishes Micro Fiction? For a long time I had this notion that most publishers prefer to publish novels and poems, while other formats tend to not find many takers. While that may be true, I think the rules only apply when there is no demand for your work. When there is no ready community that loves what you do. I think it's important to question these rules if you strongly believe in an idea. In our case, we built a community of over 2 million people across social media, organically, over four years before we published our first book with Penguin Random House India. And while Penguin has been an incredible publishing partner, we've been able to drive a bulk of the sales through a community that loves the work we do.

Where Does Micro Fiction Go From Here? The way in which Instagram opened up an ecosystem for photographers and visual storytellers, the ability to tell a story without too many words will foster an ecosystem for an entire new generation of writers. We've never seen micro fiction replace the book. In fact, it will evolve into many new interesting formats that print doesn't allow (chat fiction being one of them). That's exciting and something we look forward to everyday.

Anuj Gosalia is the Co-Founder and CEO at Terribly Tiny Tales, India's most celebrated social storytelling platform reaching over 12 million people every week. He believes in the power of stories and their ability to shape the world.

The Ghostwriter:
Gayatri Pahlajani

IT WAS at a party when someone asked me what it is I do for a living. I said I was a ghostwriter. Her eyes widened. She thought I wrote about ghosts.

While most of you are familiar with the medium, ghostwriting does not normally include writing about ghosts. While I applaud anyone who writes about ghosts, there is no amount of creative ambition in the world that would make me visit an abandoned house with a gruesome past straining my ears to hear a loud cackle at 3 AM. Having said that, it doesn't mean that ghostwriters are not haunted. Haunted by the undeniable workload, haunted by publishers and definitely haunted by the threat of genteel poverty as cheques start levitating away from them. Because submission deadlines can get pushed. As they do.

But I do love what I do.

Ghostwriters are elves to the shoemaker, the secret sauce that few readers know about. What ghostwriters essentially do is that they write all or most of the book or article behind-the-scenes either without any mention in the main credits (on book covers, for example) or any mention whatsoever. You can ghostwrite pretty much anything: from full-length books, to articles, to essays to even screenplays. And your creative involvement is either fully yours or directed by the author whose name is on the cover or in the byline.

Some of the world's biggest bestselling authors have used ghostwriters. Tom Clancy, for one, who worked with ghostwriters in part because the demand for his books far exceed any human's capacity to write them. Sheryl Sandberg in *Lean In* has credited her 'writing partner', the lesser-known Nell Scovell. And Hillary Clinton has what she calls a 'book team'. While authors rarely out their ghostwriters completely, they do give them some credit usually in mutually negotiated deals before work starts. It could be in the inside title page or in the acknowledgments section or even in a small paragraph tucked away at the back of the book. If you look hard enough, you'll find us.

But while I may have answered the question of *what*, I have not answered the question of *why*? Or, if one is prone to hyperbole, *why on earth*? Why do it? Why put in all the work only to have someone else take the credit? Why stand on the sidelines, or on the other side of the dais? What is so compelling about a profession that takes all your work but gives you little or no recognition?

Because it's fun. Because you're exposed to a variety of fields, professions, circumstances, personalities that you may otherwise not be exposed to. Because it allows you to be someone else for a little while, which enables you to get out of your own head. Because you can negotiate a staggering amount of creative freedom. Because it's intellectually challenging to write about something inaccessible like medicine or surgery and make it accessible for the lay reader. Because it gives you a platform to experiment with your writing, and chip away at it until you're ready to show it to the world. Because it buys you time to solidify your own literary identity. Because your clients are usually achievers in their own field and you get a chance to learn from the best. Because your clients' celebrity and wherewithal can push your book to the far corners of the world. Because it enables you to make a living from writing.

As a non-fiction ghostwriter, I have clapped on a hard hat and ridden a rickety elevator twenty stories high during the construction of one of India's biggest open sea bridges. I have spent years understanding physiology, brain science, motivation theory, construction technology, skin and human psychology from nutritionists, civil engineers, contractors, dermatologists, psychiatrists and surgeons, although not in that order. I've written, in turn, in the voice of a 61-year-old woman, a 59-year-old man, a 35-year-old celebrity and a forty-something expert, and my clients have been thirty years apart. I've designed psychological tests. I've constructed workbooks. I've helped Feng Shui a house. And I've watched a C-section. While taking notes.

Breadth of experience notwithstanding, there is undeniably a bit of nudge-nudge-wink-wink about hiring a ghostwriter. Not everyone agrees that its kosher: it's a *book* in someone's name. How can someone else write it? For me, my work only includes non-writers who want to educate a wider audience – in a non-fiction/self-help format – about their work and have neither the time nor the skill set for it. For example, if you're a surgeon, you're not necessarily a writer but you have a story that is worth reading. That's my job – to safely transport a concept to the other side.

The following is a glimpse into non-fiction/self-help ghostwriting for books and has been written for two sets of interested readers: one, for those who would like to engage the services of a ghostwriter. And two, briefly, for those who are looking to become ghostwriters themselves.

Let's start with the first.

When do you need a ghostwriter? It is best to approach a ghostwriter when you have a strong belief and a firm idea of what you want to convey. While prospective clients approach me even when they have a whiff of a thought, those meetings are usually not conclusive. A rule of thumb would be to author something that you would like to read yourself: a story that has either not yet been told or not told adequately. If you have a fresh spin on an old idea, that's good enough. But a sound, clear idea is important.

This sounds banal. Of course you need a strong idea. But you would be surprised by how many times I've been approached to write about a particular area of specialization but have left feeling dissatisfied with what was special about that specialization. You may want to write a book about gardening, for example, but why would people want to read it? It is only when you've answered the latter – with conviction – that you may just have a book on your hands.

It may not be easy to find a ghost who talks as it is hard for them to openly advertise their work. The best way therefore is to ask around, post messages on social media and LinkedIn, and research online. There are also literary agents that are fairly approachable that may have the names of a few good ghostwriters. If you have contacts in the publishing world, even better. But I also recommend another way to get a ghostwriter: approach one who isn't one.

This recommendation may seem like I am all beauty and not brains, but I assure you that I am the full package. My first book was a three-second consultation with my now client who I was meeting under different circumstances. It went like this:

What do you do?

I'm a writer.

Why don't you write my book?

Okay.

In short, I was asked. I was made a ghostwriter; I didn't think of becoming one. There isn't enough time in a day to read so many glorious things being written – from books to reviews to long-form journalistic pieces to op-eds to blogs to spoken word sets. If there is someone whose writing you like, approach them, especially those that you think seem accessible. Most writers publish their contact details to *be* approached. Dash off a hopeful missive articulating your wish to write your book and why they are the only one who can fulfill your desires, and see what happens. It happened to me.

At the bare minimum, the ghostwriter's responsibility extends to light/heavy research and writing the full – or a substantial part of the – book, but the extent of their role depends on both them and you. As for me, I take on full creative control: what devices I choose, what tone I adopt, what stories I want to include, how I want to position the book are all at the heart of how I ghostwrite. I also liaise with the publishing team, the client, and all other members of the village that it will undoubtedly take to produce a book, including getting the client a publisher if they don't already have one. You can be as fully involved or as hands-free as you like, and your involvement will also evolve as time goes by.

But the client has a role here too. As the author, your job is to ensure that your writer has all the tools necessary to create a good book, be it access to reading material, interviewees, resources and even submitting a skeleton of every chapter in bullet points. If it's technical or domain information, then the writer must have access to a lucid explanation – and follow-up questions – either verbally or in text. Even though you may not be actually writing it, it is this transfer of information that can sometime make you feel like you may as well do the book yourself. This could be because you're training another person to be, well, you.

Be prepared to spend a lot more time on execution than you originally thought – a book is a high-involvement project no matter who is doing the most work. If you're busy, get an assistant with technical knowledge to help you help the writer. That worked beautifully for one of my books: my submission was on schedule, and my client could get her book out on time. Everybody wins.

I have written seven books of which five have had national newsstand releases. Not one of them had a contract but this is something that works for my clients and myself personally. Whether you sign a contract also depends on the structure of your deal with the writer. I usually charge a one-time creative fee and rarely take a share of the royalties. Once the book is released, I hand over all responsibilities to the author and it's their job to parent it. But if the ghostwriter would like one, or if you would prefer one, a contract may help protect you both. A contract may also help if the information you are parting with is confidential up until the release of the book, or if the writer has access to confidential information during the process. Here, a standard NDA may just do the trick.

Be that as it may, I am equivocal about the actual power of a contract. While it occupies a rather large place in my heart, India is hardly what you would call an efficient litigious environment. Contract enforcement is notoriously difficult here so if you are seeking relief, you may sooner find it at the bottom of a bottle of single malt. Arbitration seems to be a happy medium, where disputes can be settled out of court but this too has its own associated expenses. To that end, a lot of media contracts now have arbitration clauses so you can include these in your agreements as well.

While some publishers' commission non-fiction/self-help works purely on the basis of a concept note, some insist that a few chapters be submitted along with a broad chapterization (which is all the chapters you might be including), especially for first-time authors. In these cases, you may have to get a writer on board before you find a publisher. You can also work out a piecemeal deal with the writer should the book not get commissioned at all.

Once you have a publisher in place, you would need to finalize your chapterization as well as have a creativity-killing excel sheet (or equivalent) that will help define the delivery schedule. These two become your master framework that will guide you through the length of the project.

It is only *now* that the work of actually writing the book begins.

Barring unforeseen delays, the actual book writing process takes anywhere between 4-9 months, not including the 4-10 months publishing houses take to release the book, so be prepared to have your book release one to one-and-a-half years from the time you commission the project.

Lastly, publishing houses will provide the environment for you to realize your dream of being an author but always remember that you are entirely liable for the content in your book. You will need to indemnify the publisher in case of any third-party lawsuits because they rarely take responsibility for what you have written. Be vigilant about citing work of other authors and ensure that all referencing is correct, permissions have been granted and all source material is attributed. Ensure you have your facts in place so that you avoid libel action. Even if the ghostwriter has made a mistake, it is you the author who is ultimately liable. The legal system may not be perfect, but it takes only a few hundreds of rupees to file a case. And once set in motion, it is wonderfully persistent and doesn't go away for a long time.

I've detailed the process above so you should have a fairly good idea of what it entails. But if you're genuinely interested in being a ghostwriter I can tell you that your biggest enemy is time. It takes time to craft a book that is worth publishing. It takes time to adopt your client's tone of voice. It takes time to research areas in which you have no expertise and to come off sounding like you do. You have to slip into the skin of a civil engineer, a dermatologist, an actress or a singer because you're writing for them. You have to *be* them.

And it's not just your deliverables. Because of the conflicting time schedules of your clients, your books can be delayed for no fault of yours, so you need to have the discipline both to write the book and to ensure that the book is written. Not all authors can devote a large amount of time to the project for the simple reason that they are busy people. Which is why they hired you in the first place. When deadlines are pushed, payments get delayed. To safeguard yourself, insist on an advance payment. Insist on progress payments through the process and try and finish the book on time. And have a few projects going on concurrently because post the submission of the manuscript to the publisher, there are *months* between payments. Your final dues only come in when the book goes to press.

And finally, don't write anything you're not comfortable writing. Don't sign anything you're not comfortable signing. And don't work with clients or topics you don't believe in. It is a privilege to write a book with or without your name on the cover and few things give you such a sense of achievement, more so if the book becomes a national bestseller. If you're going to ghost, be the best you can be. Put in the hours, be the thing that goes bump in the night, bypass the shortcuts and produce something of value. There are few things that feel better than being of value.

Gayatri Pahlajani holds an MSc in Gender and the Media from the London School of Economics (LSE) and works on commissioned books and films through her firm-of-one **The Big Sneeze** *(www.thebigsneeze.com) Her books are estimated to have sold nearly 100,000 copies with translations in Hindi, Bengali, Gujarati and Marathi, one of them being nominated for a Raymond Crossword Book Award. She has also recently been awarded the Women's Economic Forum's Exceptional Women of Excellence award for 2018.*

How To Make Your Book Into A Tv Series: Anand Neelakantan

IT HAPPENED during my first Jaipur Lit Fest talk in 2013. Officials from Star TV attended my session and contacted me for their then upcoming show *Siya Ke Ram*. Since my first book *Asura, Tale of the Vanquished* had become a blockbuster hit, they wanted me to write the Ravana episodes for their show. However, once I started interacting with them, they felt that I should write the entire series. That's how I broke into the TV world. I wrote around 100 episodes and its success helped me write shows like *Chakravartin Ashoka Samrat* (around 140 episodes), *Adaalat-2*, *Sankatmochan Mahabali Hanuman*, *Battle of Saragarhi*, among others, for various channels like Colours, Sony Entertainment Television and Discovery Channel.

Here's how you can make your book into a TV series, or even write for one.

The Pitch: TV show runners keep a lookout for interesting books. If they think the book is commercially viable as a TV show, they contact the author or publisher. If they think the book is not commercially viable but the writer can add value to their show, then they ask the author to become a part of the writing team without buying the book rights. This is what happened in my case. My contrarian books like *Asura* and *Ajaya* may never become mainstream shows due to the inherent nature of these books (though a few web-series are being planned on them), but my writing style and depth gave TV producers and show runners a clue on how they could use my writing skills in shows with historical and mythological themes. Alternatively, there are agents who pitch shows to producers for a fee, but this route is yet to become popular in India.

Hone Your Skills: TV is an entirely different medium from books. The transition from novelist to TV writer can be a difficult one. Screenplay writing is more of a craft than an art. The freedom a novelist enjoys is lost in writing for TV. The way a writer has to read many books to improve their writing skills, similarly a TV writer has to watch many shows to understand TV writing. TV is about entertainment, entertainment and more entertainment. It caters to a wider audience that is less sophisticated than the book reader. A certain amount of spoon-feeding is required, especially if one is writing for general entertainment channels. One has to think on one's feet as TRPs determine everything. TV is monetarily more rewarding. Writing for a web series is more like writing for a novel, but screenplay craft and dialogues are skills that need to be honed everyday. Frankly, what you write depends so much on TRPs that after some time the author has no control over the content! The customer will decide what the story will be, and this is frightening and exhilarating at the same time. This also leads to a lot of nonsense and hubris in content, as you may see on any TV channel today. Personally, I get more satisfaction while writing a novel and more thrills while writing a TV show.

What Channels To Approach: All TV channels are on the lookout for books that they can convert into a show. Romance, chick lit, humour, and crime are sought after genres by general entertainment channels like Star or Sony. Mythological fiction is not as sought after but writers can come on board as consultants or screenplay writers. Writers like Devdutt Pattanaik provide consultancy, while writers like Ashok Banker and myself provide the story, screenplay, and some consultancy too. International web channels prefer books that are more literary in nature or that have a huge brand name like Baahubali. For example, my book *The Rise of Sivagami* (based on Baahubali) is coming out as an international web series.

How To Approach Channels: You can approach production houses since TV channels generally do not accept unsolicited material. Do register your content with the Screenwriters Association. A non-published writer can also register their content for a small fee. We are living in interesting times as the web series world is opening up. With Netflix and Amazon it's easier for an author to have their work on TV, provided their writing meets their requirement. Sometimes, general entertainment channels can be a more rewarding space for writers, since the market is huge in India. Web channels will take a long time to match them.

Negotiate Good Payment: You've all heard that you get paid better for writing a TV show than you would for a book. But if you compare the number of words to payment, novels are more rewarding. In India, the screenplay writer does not get the IPR (intellectual property rights). So, once the writer gets paid for the script, they do not earn anything more. My books like *Asura* or *Ajaya* still provide me a decent living, while TV shows that have become huge hits stopped giving me payment after going off air. Still, TV is good for instant money. What one makes in a show that runs for three months is equivalent to what a mega bestselling book like *Asura* makes in two years. However, *Asura* is still in the bestseller list in its seventh year and will continue to earn me a tidy sum for the next fifty years or more. Therefore, in the long run, books beat TV hands down, if you have a bestseller! This may change, of course, once IPR becomes applicable. Moreover, books give the writer immense satisfaction and a sense of accomplishment. TV is a team sport and a writer is just one among many who makes the show successful.

The Next Step: I have started producing shows and this is the next step after writing for TV shows. And, of course, you can begin writing for movies, which is another world altogether!

To sum it up, TV is an adrenaline rush, an addiction, which is difficult to quit once you're sucked into it. Writing novels or short stories is like mediation. One can enjoy both.

Anand Neelakantan has authored three fiction books based on the epics of Ramayana and Mahabharata, including the Baahubali book series, Rise of Sivagami, Asura: Roll of the Dice, and Rise of Kali.

Epilogue:
My Writing Journey

IT WAS not turning out to be a good day. My hands were frozen from New York's biting cold. I was late to catch my train from Penn Station. And the plastic bag carrying my lunch had ripped. As I mulled over how best to salvage the remains, someone put their hand on my shoulder. I turned around and saw an old Indian lady, with hair like moonlight, smiling at me. She held out a plastic bag. When I hugged her in gratitude, she led me by the hand to a bench outside JCPenney store, where a group of her friends—other elderly Indians—were sitting. They all gathered around me, at once curious about this girl living alone in Manhattan, trying to be a writer. "Why aren't you home with your grandchildren?" I asked them. The quiet in their smiles, their long excuses, those sad lonely eyes revealed that they were not welcome at their own children's homes. I saw life etched wearily on their wrinkles and understood what they'd left unsaid. I knew I had a story.

I was 19 when my first short story, *Aberration*, was published online. But the discipline of writing, its stark loneliness, does not usually appeal to the young and skittish. I packed away the dream of being a writer. By the time I was in my mid-20s, I had already quit a lucrative job in corporate finance to pursue a dynamic, though fluid, career in broadcast journalism. I had already taken many risks in life, gone downwards in the financial graph that my friends were scaling up in. Writing would make my life worse. It was an axe of insecurity hanging above my head. I couldn't become a writer. I couldn't take that chance.

But I did. The Manhattan incident became a turning point in my life. The plot and the characters stayed with me for so many months that I finally gathered the wherewithal to write a short story called *Lemon & Chilli*. From the vantage point of those old eyes, those untold tales, I shone the light on those dark corners of our lives that we keep hidden.

This was 2008. This was when I found out that I couldn't stop writing. Writing became that raw savage beast that I walked alongside with. I loved it! But I wasn't sure if I was any good at it. So I spend the next three years honing my skills by furiously writing short stories. To improve my craft I took several writing courses in New York City.

It was insane. I was working non-stop, filling the days with a job with which to pay the bills, and writing like a maniac during every free moment. I became so consumed by my writing that I could no longer sit through a movie or a TV show, or go out for dinner or parties, as I'd feel guilty about wasting time. My social life dwindled to ten per cent of what it used to be, and I'm lucky that my deepest friendships were formed before I started writing, so I still have a strong support system. If I somehow did go out, I was so busy observing people and making mental notes that I often forgot to enjoy myself. I once had my laptop tip over and cut my upper lip (I'm a horizontal writer), and I didn't get up till my T-shirt was bloody because I was in the middle of writing a crucial scene!

After a fair share of rejections my short stories began to be published in reputed U.S. literary magazines. *Lemon & Chilli* was the first. The idea for a full-length novel, *One & A Half Wife*, came only in 2010, and that's around the time I started putting together short stories that would come together in the collection *Happy Birthday!*

Finally, I was a storyteller. But it didn't feel like something unusual to me.

This was because my childhood had been abundant with stories and books. At home, we spoke about ideas, we discussed books and we were always sharing anecdotes. I read anything that I could get my hands on. I would wonder: how long did Ayn Rand take to finish *Atlas Shrugged*, what inspired George Orwell to write *1984*, how did characters like Jane Eyre and Tom Sawyer come to life? Every time I read something brilliant, I wanted to write something brilliant. So when the time came to write, I wrote like the kind of writer I imagined my icons to be. I became the author I used to read about. I drew inspiration from my life, of being born in the beautiful hill station of Shimla, spending my childhood in Delhi, my teenage years in Mumbai, most of my 20s and early 30s living around the world like a nomad.

After my two books were ready, I spend months researching how to get them published. By this time I was living in Dubai. One fine morning on 11th January 2011 (I believe in the lucky charm of 111), I bunked work, went to a café and emailed the manuscript of *One & A Half Wife* to all the Indian publishers. Before I'd even finished my (ok, third) cup of coffee, I got a reply from Prita Maitra from Westland to say that she was really enjoying reading my novel. In two days she said she loved it enough to sign me on. *One & A Half Wife* was published in May 2012. The lovely Meru Gokhale from Random House India then published *Happy Birthday* in July 2013. Such kind of confidence in a new author was really inspiring and, honestly, a big relief.

The journey became more magical. Authors I grew up reading or revered—like Chitra Banerjee Divakaruni, Jerry Pinto, Jeet Thayil, Ashwin Sanghi and Namita Gokhale—gave my books fantastic blurbs. I remember crying tears of joy. What an honour! I won awards. I got invited to lit fests. I made many author friends. Since my two books came out within fourteen months of each other, for two years I woke up almost every day to reviewers, friends and readers saying they loved the novel and the stories. The amount of discipline, hard work and sacrifice that had gone into reaching that stage as an author made it all humbling and exhilarating.

Now, as a full-time writer, I've made my hobby a career. Frankly, I have no choice in the matter.

Writing for me is like breathing; I can't stop doing it even if I try.